# CHILDREN'S
# ENCYCLOPEDIA
## OF PHYSICS

## Tom Jackson

ARCTURUS

## Picture Credits:

Every attempt has been made to clear copyright. Should there be any inadvertent omission, please apply to the publisher for rectification.

Key: b-bottom, t-top, c-center, l-left, r-right
cover main Open Studi0/Shutterstock, tl ShutterStockStudio/Shutterstock, tlc Master1305/Shutterstock, tc ALPS DESIGN/Shutterstock, tcr VIZ UALNI/Shutterstock, tr Johan Swanepoel/Shutterstock, back cover Sky Antonio/Shutterstock, inside front cover artjazz/Shutterstock, inside back cover Maridav/Shutterstock;6–7c Stock Rocket/Shutterstock;6 cl Aygul Sarvarova/Shutterstock Page6br Sirocco/Shutterstock;7tr Wikimedia Commons;8–9c nobeastsofierce/Shutterstock;8c KenAge/Shutterstock;9bc Lukasz Pawel Szczepanski/Shutterstock.;8br Wikimedia Commons;10–11c marilook/Shutterstock;10c OSweetNature/Shutterstock;10bl Standret/Shutterstock;10br Milan Sommer/Shutterstock;11br Wikimedia Commons;12–13c JoeSAPhotos/Shutterstock;12c Pixel B/Shutterstock Page12bl Anatoliy Sadovskiy/Shutterstock;13br Wikimedia Commons;14–15c New Africa/Shutterstock;14cr paul ridsdale/Alamy Stock Photo;15bl Roman Samborskyi/Shutterstock;15br Wikimedia Commons;16–17c Sky Antonio/Shutterstock;16cl Kirschner/Shutterstock;16br Morphart Creation/Shutterstock;17tr Wikimedia Commons;18–19c Simon Balson/Alamy Stock Photo;19tc Artsiom P/Shutterstock;18c StockCanarias/Shutterstock;18br BorderlineRebel/Wikimedia Commons;20–21c Coolakov_com/Shutterstock;20cl Oliver Furrer/Alamy Stock Photo;20br Rabilal poudel/Shutterstock;21tr LeManna/Shutterstock;22–23c New Africa/Shutterstock;22 cr Gonzalo Buzonni/Shutterstock;22bl Stas Moroz/Shutterstock.;23br Palace of Versailles/Wikimedia Commons;24–25c solarseven/Shutterstock;24cl petrroudny43/Shutterstock;24br CERN/Science Photo Library;25br KPNO/NOIRLab/NSF/AURA/Wikimedia Commons;26–27c Wut.Anunai/Shutterstock;26cl Rodrigo Garrido/Shutterstock;27t Benoist/Shutterstock;26 br Wikimedia Commons;28–29c Paul Hennessy/Alamy Stock Photo;28cr Colin Underhill/Alamy Stock Photo;28bl BrainCityArts/Shutterstock;29 br Wikimedia Commons;30–31c Dennis Cox/Alamy Stock Photo;30cl BiniClick/Shutterstock;31tr Dejan Dundjerski/Shutterstock;30 br MRC Laboratory of Molecular Biology/Wikimedia Commons;32–33c Littlekidmoment/Shutterstock;32cl Arina P Habich/Shutterstock;32bc artjazz/Shuttterstock;32br Wikimedia Commons;34–35c Grindstone Media Group/Shutterstock;34cl Getty Images/salihkilic;35br Aerial-motion/Shutterstock;34br Wikimedia Commons;36–37c BearFotos/Shutterstock;36c Melnikov Dmitriy/Alamy Stock Photo;37cr Designua/Shutterstock;36br Wikimedia Commons;38–39c kelifamily/Shutterstock;38cl Marina Plevako/Shutterstock;39tr Pepermpron/Shutterstock;38br Wikimedia Commons;40–41c Stocktrek Images, Inc./Alamy Stock Photo;40cr Germanskydiver/Shutterstock;40bl Drawing For Freedom/Shutterstock;41br Wikimedia Commons;42–43c Mark Davidson/Alamy Stock Photo;42cr Mark Agnor/Shutterstock;42bc Paopano/Shutterstock;43tr Wikimedia Commons;44–45c Dee Adams/Alamy Stock Photo;44c Dimitrios Karamitros/Shutterstock;45tl Chris Sattleberger/Science Photo Library;44br Wikimedia Commons;p46–47c Sven Hansche/Shutterstock p46tl Pat_Hastings/Shutterstock p46cl Tang Yan Song/Shutterstock p46b A;le Zoom Zoom/Shutterstock p47b The Picture Art Collection/Alamy;48–49c Jake Lyell/Alamy Stock Photo;48c hedgehog96/Shutterstock;48br Maridav/Shutterstock;49tr Wikimedia Commons;50cl 2DAssets/Shutterstock;50c Angelaoblak/Shutterstock;50bl Tomas Ragina/Shutterstock;50br Wikimedia Commons;52–53c txking/shutterstock;52cl Rupendra Sing Rawat/Shutterstock;52br JoeSAPhotos/Shutterstock;53br Wikimedia Commons;54–55c Lianys/Shutterstock;54cl Mike Flippo/Shutterstock;54br Friends Stock/Shutterstock;55tr Colport/Alamy Stock Photo;56–57c Monkey Business Images/Shutterstock;56cl StoryTime Studio/Shutterstock;57tl PeopleImages.com Yuri A/shutterstock;56bl Pictorial Press Ltd/Alamy Stock Photo;58–59c RobSt/Shutterstock;58c P Greenwood Photography/Shutterstock;59cr sirtravelalot/Shutterstock;58br Wikimedia Commons;60–61c Koto Images/Shutterstock;60c BearFotos/Shutterstock;60bl Rawpixel.com/Shutterstock;61br Wikimedia Commons;62–63 Shcherbakov Ilya/Shutterstock;62cl ClassicStock/Alamy Stock Photo;62br Starodubtsev Konstantin/Shutterstock;63tr Wikimedia Commons;64–65c Xmentoys/Shutterstock;64c BlueRingMedia/Shutterstock;65tr Artur Didyk/Shutterstock;64br s.dali/Shutterstock;66–67c US Navy Photo/Alamy Stock Photo;66cl Nick Fox/Shutterstock;66br GLYPHstock/Shutterstock;67tr Wikimedia Commons;68–69c AlexLMX/shutterstock;68tcl George Howard Jr/shutterstock;69tl Conspectus/Alamy Stock Photo;68br GoXxu Chocolate/Shutterstock;70–71c Christian Bertrand/Shutterstock;71br petrroudny43/Shutterstock;70c EpicStockMedia/Shutterstock;70 Wikimedia Commons;72–73c ONYXprj/Shutterstock;72cl Subbotina Anna/Shutterstock;72br michaeljung/Shutterstock;73tr Wikimedia Commons;74–75c VeeJey/Shutterstock;74c Nutkins.J/Shutterstock;75bc Natee Meepian/Shutterstock;74br Wikimedia Commons;76–77c Anton Brehov/Shutterstock;76bc David R. Frazier Photolibrary, Inc./Alamy Stock Photo;76cl tersetki/Shutterstock;77br Michel Bakni/Wikimedia Commons;78–79c Kuki Ladron de Guevara/Shutterstock;78cl VectorMine/Shutterstock;77br sree rag/Shutterstock;78tr Science Photo Library;80–81c EternalMoments/Shutterstock;80c Hannah Spray Photography/Shutterstock;80bl Smeerjewegproducties/Shutterstock;81br IanDagnall Computing/Alamy Stock Photo;82–81c Ollyy/Shutterstock;82cl KRPD/Shutterstock;82br kotikoti/Shutterstock;81tr Wikimedia Commons;84–85c Sheila Terry/Science Photo Library;84cr Honourr/Shutterstock;84bl kckate16/Shutterstock;85br Wikimedia Commons;86–87c K.H.Kjeldsen/Science Photo Library;86cl VectorMine/Shutterstock;87tc voronaman/Shutterstock;86br Rattiya Thongdumhyu/Shutterstock;88–89c sciencephotos/Alamy Stock Photo;88cl Johan Swanepoel/Shutterstock;88br New Africa/Shutterstock;89br Wikimedia Commons;90–91c NewSs/Shutterstock;90cr Billion Photos/Shutterstock;90bl VectorMine/Shutterstock;91tr Wikimedia Commons;92–93c Vershinin91/Shutterstock;92c VectorMine/Shutterstock;93tl petrroudny43/Shutterstock;92br Wikimedia Commons;94–95c La;o Alexander/Shutterstock;94cl Ferenc Szelepcsenyi/Alamy Stock Photo;94br Andrewshots/Shutterstock;95br Wikimedia Commons;96–97c Dragon Images/Shutterstock;96cl Bespaliy/Shutterstock;97c Dream01/Shutterstock 97br Wikimedia Commons;98–99c ronstik/Shutterstock;98c huntingSHARK/Shutterstock;98bl huntingSHARK/Shutterstock;99tr Science History Images/Alamy Stock Photo;100–101c Ground Picture/Shutterstock;100cl BLKstudio/Shutterstock;100br Steve Cukrov/Shutterstock;101tr Wikimedia Commons;102–103c asharkyu/Shutterstock;102cr Designua/Shutterstock;102bl Designua/Shutterstock;103br Everett Collection/Shutterstock;104–105 Gerry H/Shutterstock;104c Designua/Shutterstock;105tr Simon Annable/Shutterstock;104br Wikimedia Commons;106–107c ssuaphotos/Shutterstock;106c zstock/Shutterstock;106bl Evgeny_V/Shutterstock;107tr Wikimedia Commons;108–109c Grzegorz Czapski/Shutterstock;108cl Rainbow06/Shutterstock;108cr Dn Br/Shutterstock;109tr Peter Sobolev/Shutterstock;108br Wikimedia Commons;110–111c Sochillplanets/Shutterstock;110c rapisan sawangphon/Alamy Stock Photo;110bl aslysun/Shutterstock;110br IM Imagery/Shutterstock; ;112–113c Siberian Art/Shutterstock;112cl 3000ad/Shutterstock;113bl NASA/Ames/JPL-Caltech;112br NASA;114–115c Triff/Shutterstock;114c Designua/Shutterstock;114bl Macrovector/Shutterstock;115br Wikimedia Commons;116–117c Fernando Astasio Avila/Shutterstock;116cl NASA;116br Jacques Dayan/Shutterstock;117tr Gelderen, Hugo van/Anefo/ Wikimedia Commons;118–119c Mark Garlick/Alamy Stock Photo;118cl MarcelClemens/Shutterstock;118br Aphelleon/Shutterstock;119br Wikimedia Commons;120–121c Alan Dyer/VWPics/ Alamy Stock Photo;120cr 24K-Production/Shutterstock;120bl Amanda J Dorton/Shutterstock;121tr Wikimedia Commons;122–123c rukawajung/Shutterstock;122cl Wikimedia Commons;123cr ChiccoDodiFC/Shutterstock;122br Wikimedia Commons;124–125c hakan2554/Shutterstock;124c Sasin Paraksa/Shutterstock;125tc Sam Chivers, Debut Art/Science Photo Library;125br Wikimedia Commons; Sky Antonio/Shutterstock artjazz/Shutterstock Maridav/Shutterstock;4–5c a katz/Shutterstock;4cr D-Visions/Shutterstock;4br Smile Fight/Shutterstock;5tl Supamotionstock.com/Shutterstock;5bl JAVS/Shutterstock;122–123c pixelparticle/Shutterstock;122cr Designua/Shutterstock;122bl 24K-Production/Shutterstock;123br Wikimedia Commons

ARCTURUS

This edition published in 2024 by Arcturus Publishing Limited
26/27 Bickels Yard, 151–153 Bermondsey Street,
London SE1 3HA

Copyright © Arcturus Holdings Limited

Author: Tom Jackson
Consultants: Anne Rooney and Robert Snedden
Designer: Lorraine Inglis
Picture research: Lorraine Inglis and Paul Futcher
Editors: Donna Gregory and Becca Clunes
Design manager: Rosie Bellwood
Managing editor: Joe Harris

ISBN: 978-1-3988-4383-7
CH011574US
Supplier 26, Date 0724, Print run 00007026

Printed in China

# CONTENTS

Introduction                                        4

## Chapter 1:
## Forces and Matter                                6

What Is Matter?                                     6
Inside Atoms                                        8
Radioactivity                                      10
Electromagnetism                                   12
Magnets                                            14
Gravity                                            16
Weight and Mass                                    18
Friction and Drag                                  20
Pressure                                           22
Dark Matter                                        24

## Chapter 2:
## Motion                                          26

First Law of Motion                                26
Second Law of Motion                               28
Third Law of Motion                                30
Momentum                                           32
Velocity and Acceleration                          34
Oscillation                                        36
Rotational Motion                                  38
Orbits and Weightlessness                          40
Ballistics                                         42
Flight                                             44
Buoyancy                                           46

## Chapter 3:
## Understanding Energy                            48

Doing Work                                         48
Thermal Energy                                     50
Kinetic Energy                                     52
Potential Energy                                   54
Other Types of Energy                              56
Power                                              58
Levers                                             60
Ramps and Screws                                   62
Wheels and Pulleys                                 64
Engines                                            66

## Chapter 4:
## Waves and Optics                                68

Properties of a Wave                               68
Types of Waves                                     70
Electromagnetic Spectrum                           72
Interference                                       74
Reflection                                         76
Refraction                                         78
Lenses                                             80
Distortion and Diffraction                         82
Telescopes                                         84
Microscopes                                        86

## Chapter 5:
## Electricity                                     88

What Is Electricity?                               88
Conductors and Insulators                          90
Current                                            92
Voltage                                            94
Ohm's Law                                          96
Circuits                                           98
Electrical Components                             100
Light Bulbs                                       102
Electric Power                                    104
Renewable Power                                   106
Electronics                                       108
Microchips                                        110

## Chapter 6:
## Stars and Space                                112

The Solar System                                  112
Stars                                             114
The Moon                                          116
The Planets                                       118
Comets and Asteroids                              120
Galaxies                                          122
Space and Time                                    124

GLOSSARY                                          126
INDEX                                             128

# Introduction

Science is all about learning and understanding the rules that make the Universe and everything in it work. At the heart of this is physics, the science of matter, the stuff from which everything is made, and the energy that moves and transforms that matter. Understanding physics allows us to explain how everything else works.

## Forces and Motion

Physics sets out laws of motion that explain how things move. These acrobats are expert movers. They are relying on physics to put on their show. These laws look at the mass of an object—a measure of how much matter is inside it—and the size and direction of the forces pushing on it.

## Investigating Matter

Matter is made up of tiny building blocks called atoms, which are in turn made from even smaller subatomic particles. Physicists use huge machines called particle accelerators that smash atoms together at enormous speed to reveal their hidden structure.

## Electricity and Magnets

One of the most important discoveries of physics was that electricity and magnetism were linked together. Electric currents generate magnetism and magnetism generates electricity. This knowledge led to electric motors and generators and to the many gadgets such as computers, televisions, and smartphones we use every day.

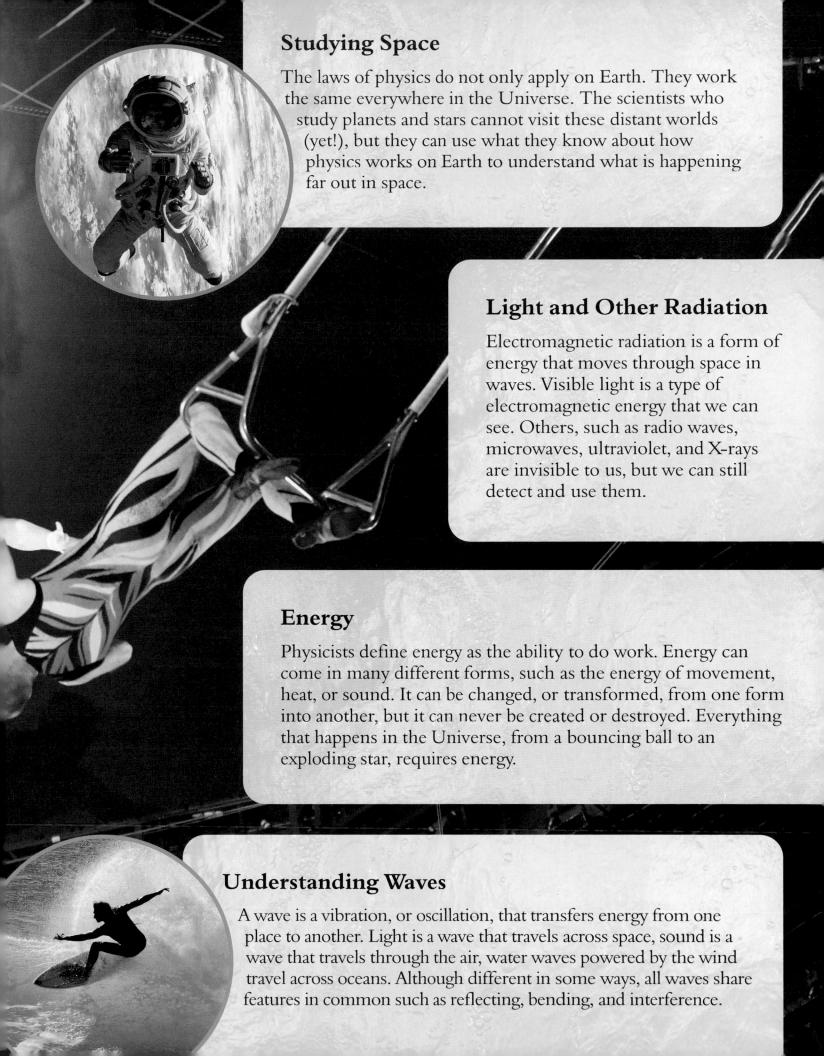

## Studying Space

The laws of physics do not only apply on Earth. They work the same everywhere in the Universe. The scientists who study planets and stars cannot visit these distant worlds (yet!), but they can use what they know about how physics works on Earth to understand what is happening far out in space.

## Light and Other Radiation

Electromagnetic radiation is a form of energy that moves through space in waves. Visible light is a type of electromagnetic energy that we can see. Others, such as radio waves, microwaves, ultraviolet, and X-rays are invisible to us, but we can still detect and use them.

## Energy

Physicists define energy as the ability to do work. Energy can come in many different forms, such as the energy of movement, heat, or sound. It can be changed, or transformed, from one form into another, but it can never be created or destroyed. Everything that happens in the Universe, from a bouncing ball to an exploding star, requires energy.

## Understanding Waves

A wave is a vibration, or oscillation, that transfers energy from one place to another. Light is a wave that travels across space, sound is a wave that travels through the air, water waves powered by the wind travel across oceans. Although different in some ways, all waves share features in common such as reflecting, bending, and interference.

# What Is Matter?

Matter is anything that takes up space and has mass. All matter is made of tiny particles called atoms. Your body, your home, and the trees, oceans, rocks, and everything else on planet Earth are all made of matter. There are different kinds of energy, but they are not types of matter. They don't take up space or have mass.

Although we cannot see it, we are surrounded by matter all the time. These are the gases in the air!

## States of Matter

Matter exists in three main states—solid, liquid, and gas. The state is the result of how atoms can move within the matter. Matter changes state as it becomes hotter or colder. In a cold solid, the atoms are arranged into a fixed shape and volume. Solids melt into liquids as they warm up. Liquids have a fixed volume but no fixed shape. Heating a liquid until it boils makes a gas, which has neither a fixed shape nor volume.

The most familiar matter that changes between solid, liquid, and gas is water. On Earth, it is solid as ice, liquid as water, and gas as steam.

## Matter and Energy

When matter is heated, the heat energy makes the atoms vibrate. As matter cools—loses heat—the atoms move less. A change of state is a physical change, because the matter remains the same substance. Atoms in it remain joined in the same way but are in different places. Matter can also lose or gain energy in a chemical change. A chemical change rearranges the atoms into different substances. For example, burning a log changes it from wood to smoke, gas, and ash.

An explosion is a rapid chemical change that changes the nature of the matter. Some is converted to smoke or gases. A lot of energy is released as heat.

**DID YOU KNOW?** There is a fourth state of matter called plasma. It can be created when a gas gets very hot, or is affected by electricity. The Sun is made from plasma. In fact, 99 percent of all known matter in the Universe is plasma!

## HALL OF FAME:
### John Dalton
#### 1766–1844

The idea of matter being made of atoms dates back to ancient Greece. Dalton, a scientist from Britain, introduced modern atomic theory in 1801. He suggested that atoms of different types combine to make different substances. They always combine in the same proportions to make the same new substance.

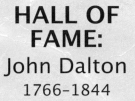

Matter can be pushed and pulled on by forces. The forces can make the matter move and change shape.

Matter exists as millions of different substances. Each substance has its own properties, such as color, density, and stretchiness.

# Inside Atoms

There are 118 chemical elements (simple substances like carbon and gold) that are the ingredients of all other matter. Each element has its own unique type of atom. An atom is a tiny particle that is far too small to see. Atoms differ in the number of subatomic particles they contain.

Electrons have a negative charge and they move around the outside the atom. An atom has the same number of electrons and protons.

## Smaller Particles

We used to think atoms were indivisible—they couldn't be broken down—but now physicists know they are made up of smaller subatomic particles. Each atom has a nucleus in the middle, which has roughly equal numbers of protons and neutrons. Electrons whiz around the nucleus. Most of the volume of an atom is empty space. The width of an atom is more than 10,000 times the width of its nucleus. Even the neutrons and protons are made of smaller particles, called quarks. There are three quarks in each neutron or proton.

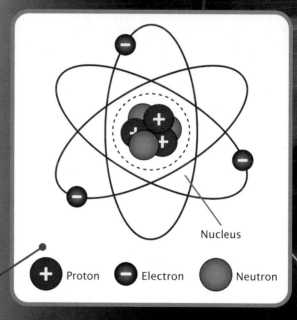

Nucleus

+ Proton  − Electron  ● Neutron

In reality, the electrons are much farther from the nucleus than this!

**HALL OF FAME:**
Ernest Rutherford
1871–1937

This scientist from New Zealand became one of the first atomic physicists. In 1911, he led the team that discovered that atoms have a compact nucleus and a lot of empty space, and that the positive charge of an atom is concentrated in the nucleus. In 1997, an element with 104 protons was named Rutherfordium in his honor.

**DID YOU KNOW?** An atom is approximately 0.2 to 0.5 nanometers across. A nanometer is a billionth of a meter. Around 5 million large atoms could line up across this dot . which is about 1 mm (0.04 inches) wide.

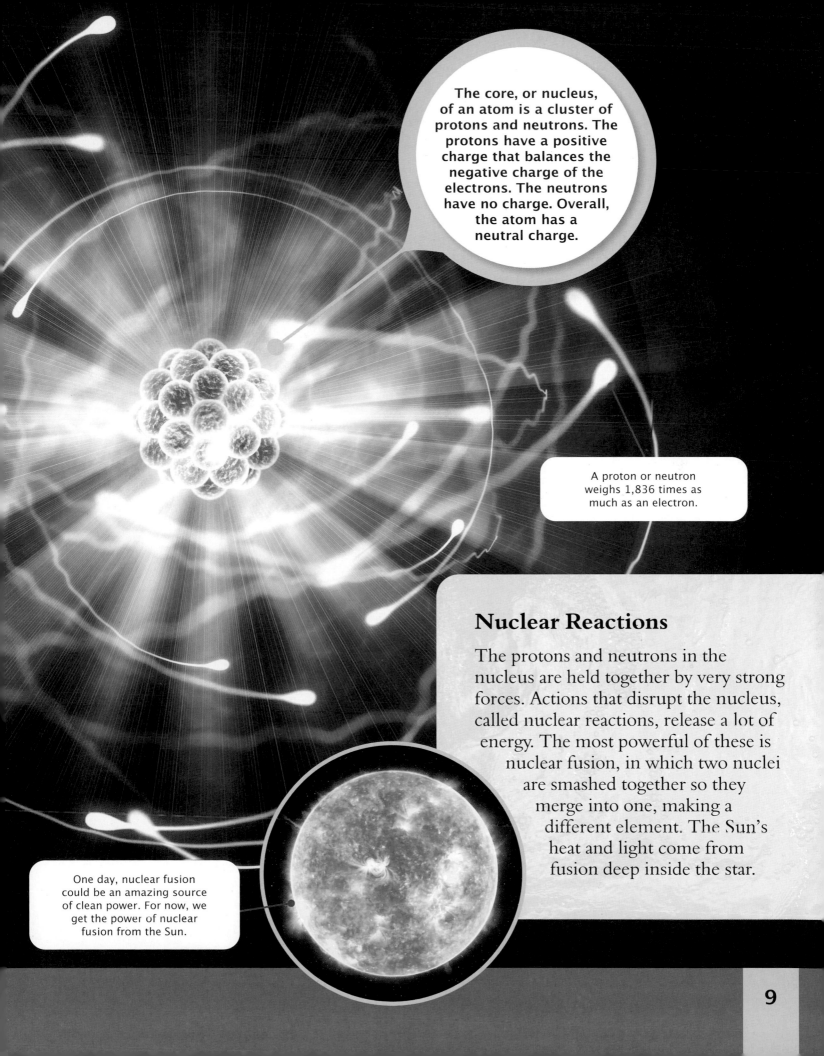

The core, or nucleus, of an atom is a cluster of protons and neutrons. The protons have a positive charge that balances the negative charge of the electrons. The neutrons have no charge. Overall, the atom has a neutral charge.

A proton or neutron weighs 1,836 times as much as an electron.

## Nuclear Reactions

The protons and neutrons in the nucleus are held together by very strong forces. Actions that disrupt the nucleus, called nuclear reactions, release a lot of energy. The most powerful of these is nuclear fusion, in which two nuclei are smashed together so they merge into one, making a different element. The Sun's heat and light come from fusion deep inside the star.

One day, nuclear fusion could be an amazing source of clean power. For now, we get the power of nuclear fusion from the Sun.

# Radioactivity

Many atoms are stable and stay the same forever. But some large atoms have so many protons and neutrons that the nucleus tends to fall apart. The process of unstable atoms coming apart is called radioactivity. Radioactivity releases particles and energy, which can be used in medicine and as a source of power.

Nuclear power stations use the heat from decaying radioactive fuel to make electricity. The process uses a nuclear reaction called fission, where unstable atoms split apart, releasing heat and other radiation.

## Radioactive Decay

Radioactive elements change through a process called radioactive decay. The unstable nucleus pushes out particles to make itself more stable. Changing the number of protons in the nucleus transforms an atom from one element to another. For example, uranium atoms decay into thorium atoms. The decay process stops when an atom reaches a stable form.

Alpha decay happens when the nucleus throws out two protons and two neutrons, called an alpha particle. In beta decay, it releases an electron, changing a neutron to a proton. A third type, gamma radiation, is produced when the radioactive nucleus puts out waves of energy called gamma rays.

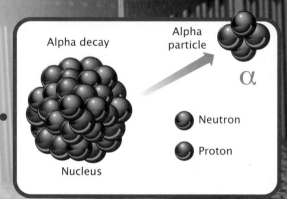

Alpha decay

Alpha particle

$\alpha$

Neutron

Proton

Nucleus

## Dangers of Radiation

Radioactive substances are dangerous and must be handled with care, as the energy released by decay can damage living cells. People who work with radioactive material must wear protective suits to block these particles. As well as two types of particles (alpha and beta), decay releases high-energy radiation, like X-rays and gamma rays. These can be blocked by thick metal and concrete.

This sign warns that radioactive substances are present in the area. Safety equipment should be used.

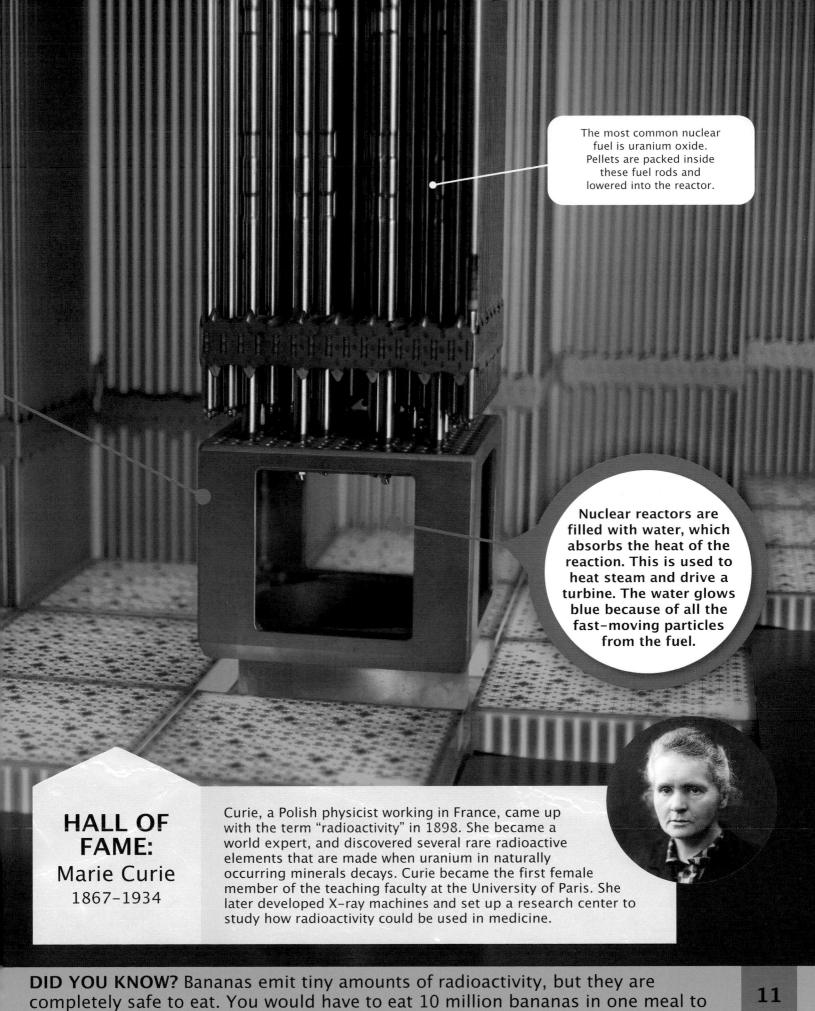

The most common nuclear fuel is uranium oxide. Pellets are packed inside these fuel rods and lowered into the reactor.

Nuclear reactors are filled with water, which absorbs the heat of the reaction. This is used to heat steam and drive a turbine. The water glows blue because of all the fast-moving particles from the fuel.

**HALL OF FAME:**
Marie Curie
1867–1934

Curie, a Polish physicist working in France, came up with the term "radioactivity" in 1898. She became a world expert, and discovered several rare radioactive elements that are made when uranium in naturally occurring minerals decays. Curie became the first female member of the teaching faculty at the University of Paris. She later developed X-ray machines and set up a research center to study how radioactivity could be used in medicine.

**DID YOU KNOW?** Bananas emit tiny amounts of radioactivity, but they are completely safe to eat. You would have to eat 10 million bananas in one meal to get a dangerous dose.

# Electromagnetism

Electromagnetism is one of the basic forces in the universe. It produces electricity, magnetism, and light, and it holds matter together. All particles have an electric charge, which can be positive, negative, or neutral. Objects with opposite charges are attracted to each other, while those with like charges push each other away. The charge comes from subatomic particles, most often the negatively charged electron. Anything that gains extra electrons has a negative charge, while anything that loses them has a positive charge.

## Light Radiation

Visible light, radio waves, infrared, and X-rays are all forms of electromagnetic radiation. When electrons in an atom give out energy, they release a burst of light or other radiation. When that radiation hits another atom, it might be taken in by an electron (absorbed) or bounce off again (reflected).

A laser is an instrument that can produce a powerful beam of light. The word laser stands for the scientific term that explains how a laser beam is produced: Light Amplification by the Stimulated Emission of Radiation."

## Electric Currents

Electricity is a flow of charged particles—most often electrons. The electrons move from an area where there are many electrons to a place where there are fewer. Batteries and other sources of electricity keep the current flowing by always adding more electrons at one end and removing them from the other.

Batteries use chemical reactions to produce electric currents.

**DID YOU KNOW?** The force of electromagnetism is 137 times weaker than the strong force that holds the particles of the atomic nucleus together, but many trillions of times stronger than the force of gravity.

The body's motion is powered by electromagnetic forces in the muscles. Charged particles called ions move through the muscle cells, making them change shape and contracting the muscle.

Electromagnetic force holds atoms together, keeping the negatively charged electrons bound to the positively charged nucleus.

Electromagnetic force also works between atoms, pushing the outermost electrons away from those of nearby atoms and so keeping the atoms separate. This is why the baseball bounces off the bat instead of going through it.

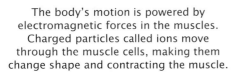

**HALL OF FAME:**
Hans Christian Ørsted
1777–1851

This Danish scientist discovered the link between electricity and magnetism, and thus created a new area of physics called electromagnetism. Ørsted discovered that the magnetic needle of a compass will swing toward a wire carrying an electric current, but then swing back to point north when the current is turned off. In 1820 he published his finding that an electric current produces a magnetic field around the wire it travels through.

13

# Magnets

Magnetism is a complex process based on how atoms are aligned inside a material. It is most obvious in metals like iron and nickel. A magnet produces a magnetic field around itself that affects how particles or objects will line up or arrange themselves. All magnets have a north pole and a south pole. Opposite poles attract each other while like poles repel each other.

## Electromagnets

There are two main types of magnet—permanent magnets and electromagnets. A permanent magnet is always magnetic. An electromagnet can have its magnetic force turned on and off. It is usually made from iron with a copper coil around it. An electric current in the coil turns the iron into a magnet, but only while the current flows. Electromagnets are very useful. For example, they can be used as parts in a machine that move when the electric current is turned on.

This scrap metal grabber is an electromagnet. It can pick up magnetic objects made of iron and move them to a different place. When the current is switched off, the iron drops to the ground.

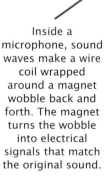

Inside a microphone, sound waves make a wire coil wrapped around a magnet wobble back and forth. The magnet turns the wobble into electrical signals that match the original sound.

## Used in Gadgets

Magnets are important parts of electrical devices. Very early computers—from long before microchips were invented—used electromagnetic switches to connect and disconnect their circuits. Magnetic storage devices, from hard disk drives to the magnetic strips on credit cards, store data as tiny positive and negative charges on a surface, coded as 0s and 1s. These are written to and read from the surface by an electromagnet.

**DID YOU KNOW?** Earth's magnetic field is created by the currents flowing through the planet's hot liquid metal core.

Magnetic forces are strongest at the poles of a magnet. There are two poles on each magnet, north and south. Like poles repel each other, and opposite poles attract each other.

A magnet is surrounded by a force field that runs from one pole to the other. Magnetic objects that enter the field are pulled toward the magnet.

Magnets have most effect on ferromagnetic materials, which include the metals iron, nickel, and cobalt. Other metals are only weakly affected by magnets, and non-metals like plastic are not affected at all.

**HALL OF FAME:**
William Gilbert
1544–1603

Gilbert was a British doctor who was once in charge of looking after the health Queen Elizabeth I, but he also carried out experiments to test his theory that Earth is a giant magnet. He carved spheres out of lodestone, a naturally magnetic, iron-rich rock. He then placed a compass on different parts of each sphere. The magnetic needle always pointed to the sphere's north pole, just as a magnetic compass points to Earth's North Pole.

# Gravity

What goes up must come down—because of the force of gravity. Gravity is a force of attraction between all objects that have mass. More massive bodies produce a stronger gravitational pull than less massive ones. The force between two objects also becomes stronger as the objects get closer together.

The force of Earth's gravity makes objects—including these skydivers—accelerate toward the middle of the planet.

## Planetary Orbits

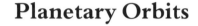

Gravity is the force that keeps a planet in orbit around a star, and moons in orbit around a planet. The gravity of the larger body—the star, for example—is pulling on the smaller one. The planet does not fall into the star because it is traveling too fast. It is falling all the time, but the direction that would take it to the star's middle (or "down") keeps changing, so it constantly "falls" around!

Jupiter has several dozen moons that are all held in place by gravity.

## Measuring Gravity

The strength of gravity acting between bodies depends on how much mass they each have. The link between a mass and the gravity it produces is a number called the gravitational constant (G), sometimes referred to as "big G." G is the same all over the Universe and can be used to calculate the pull of gravity between objects anywhere.

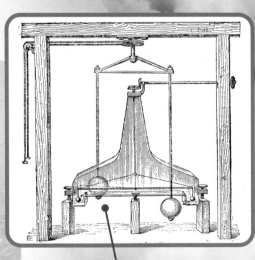

In the 1790s, Henry Cavendish measured the pull of gravity between large and small balls so he could figure out a value for G, then used the value to calculate the weight of Earth.

The law of gravity was described by Newton in the mid-seventeenth century. He had returned to his home in the country to escape an epidemic of plague. He sat in his garden and saw an apple fall from a tree to the ground. At that moment, Newton understood how gravity acts between two bodies. Newton also explained the laws of motion, studied light, and created the reflecting telescope, improving on the refracting telescopes then available.

The initial downward pull of gravity is soon balanced by the upward push of resistance from the air. The skydivers then stop accelerating, but keep falling at a constant speed called the terminal velocity.

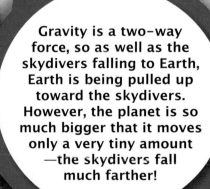

Gravity is a two-way force, so as well as the skydivers falling to Earth, Earth is being pulled up toward the skydivers. However, the planet is so much bigger that it moves only a very tiny amount —the skydivers fall much farther!

**DID YOU KNOW?** The gravitational effect of a black hole is so powerful that even light cannot escape it—and that is why it is a black hole.

# Weight and Mass

The words "weight" and "mass" are often used interchangeably, but they have different meanings. Mass is a measure of how much matter is in an object. That object's weight is the force of gravity pulling on it. On Earth, the two measures are the same, but on the Moon, where gravity is lower, an object would weigh less than on Earth. The object's mass would always be the same, however.

The mass of these weights is a fixed amount, a measure of the amount of matter in them. That never changes—even in space.

## Making Measurements

Weight and mass are measured on Earth using scales that measure the force pulling down on an object. However, mass is also a measure of how an object will resist moving. When floating in space, an object will not push down on scales at all and so it is "weightless," but its mass means it still needs a big push to get it moving—and to stop it again.

On electronic scales, the weight is measured by how much an object presses down on a pad inside.

## HALL OF FAME:
## Andrea Ghez
### 1965–

Ghez is an American astronomer who discovered the most massive thing in the galaxy. In 2012, Ghez showed that there is a black hole in the middle of the Milky Way, called Sagittarius A*. Ghez used big telescopes to watch how the gravity from the black hole made nearby stars move very fast. She used those speeds to calculate the pull of gravity from the black hole, which told her that Sagittarius A* had a mass 4 million times that of the Sun!

**DID YOU KNOW?** The pilots of fast fighter jets experience G-force as they make tight turns. A G-force of 2 is twice the natural pull of Earth's gravity, so the pilot's body weighs twice as much.

An astronaut in space is weightless but not massless.

## Weightless in Space

Astronauts on the International Space Station have no weight, since they are in constant freefall, but they need to monitor their mass to make sure they stay healthy. This is measured using a special device that calculates how much force is needed to move their body against a spring of known resistance. An object with mass still needs force to move it, even when it has no weight.

The weightlifter has to create a force greater than gravity to get the weight off the ground and above her head.

The weight of this bar depends on the force of gravity pulling it down to the ground. On Jupiter, where the gravity is stronger, its weight would be nearly three times as much!

# Friction and Drag

Matter is seldom smooth, and is always rubbing against other matter—even at the atomic level. This rubbing creates resistance forces called friction and drag. Friction occurs when two solids resist moving against each other, while drag is the resistance of an object moving through a liquid or gas.

Friction is reduced by lubricants. These are usually liquids that form a slippery layer between the solid surfaces. This reduces how much the surfaces rub, and so means there is less friction.

## Air Resistance

When an aircraft moves through the air, the air rushing around it works against the force moving the craft forward. This creates drag, or air resistance, that slows it. When an object is falling, drag slows its fall. The size of the drag force depends on the surface area of the object. A wide but light object like a feather flutters through the air, but a heavy and pointed object like a spear slices through it with little drag.

A parachute has a very large surface area, which creates a large drag force. The drag reduces the speed of the fall so a person can land safely.

## Rough Surfaces

Friction is produced when solid objects slide past each other. The rough surfaces will snag on each other and hamper the sliding motion. Friction is present in all moving parts and is why machines always grind to halt unless they are given another push.

The treads on a tractor wheel are designed to create a large friction force so they grab the ground even in slippery conditions.

# HALL OF FAME:
## Agnès Poulbot
### 1967–

This French engineer is one of the world's leading designers of car tires. With her colleague, Jacques Barraud, she designed tires with layers of shallow tread that grip the road and channel water away from the wheel. As one layer wears away, a new layer is revealed, restoring the tire's grip. Good tires mean the car uses less energy to move forward, so it is more fuel-efficient.

Ice skates have a thin blade, so there is little contact between the skate and the ice. The blade and ice are both smooth, and a thin layer of liquid water lubricates the movement, making it almost frictionless.

Each liquid has a particular "runniness" or viscosity. Water has a low viscosity so it produces less drag and friction. Honey is a liquid with a much higher viscosity and so it would be much harder to skate over!

**DID YOU KNOW?** Shooting stars are little rocks from space that burn up in the high atmosphere. They burn because the strong air resistance makes them very hot.

# Pressure

Pressure measures the amount of force working in a specific area. In an area of high pressure, a large force is working in a small area. The same force acting in a wider area makes a lower pressure.

The air in a car tire is around 2.5 times higher than the normal air pressure. That high-pressure air inside makes the tire stiff but still allows it to bend when needed.

## Atmospheric Pressure

The air around us is not weightless. Instead, it is pushing down on the ground (and us) all the time. This is measured as atmospheric pressure (also known as air pressure). Standard air pressure is equivalent to the weight of several large pitchers of water pushing onto every inch of your skin. Your body is used to this pressure—it's normal.

Air pressure is linked to weather changes. When the pressure drops, a storm is coming.

Scuba divers can only go to about 40 m (130 ft) underwater. After that, the pressure pushing on the body makes it too hard for air from the tanks to get into a diver's lungs.

## Water Pressure

Water is denser than air, so the pressure from water is much greater. At the ocean's surface a swimmer experiences normal air pressure. If they swim down 10 m (33 ft), that pressure will have doubled as the weight of the water pushes on the body. In the deepest parts of the ocean, the pressure is so high that it would squash the body completely. Only the toughest submersibles can visit there.

**DID YOU KNOW?** Air pressure is lower at higher altitudes because the air is less dense. At the top of Mount Everest the air pressure is only one-third of the pressure at sea level.

A pump is a machine that pushes liquids or gases. The air pump used here keeps pushing air into the tire to increase the pressure.

A one-way valve allows the air to flow into the tire, but stops it from blowing out again.

## HALL OF FAME:
Blaise Pascal
1623–1662

This French mathematician and physicist made the first measurements of air pressure and explained how it worked. As a result, the scientific unit of pressure is the pascal (Pa). Normal air pressure at sea level is 100,000 Pa. Pascal also helped create the mathematics of probability, which uses numbers to figure out how likely it is that something will happen.

# Dark Matter

Astronomers have measured all of the matter in the Universe that they can see—all of the stars and galaxies—but they have found that the mass of the Universe is much greater than the total mass of all of the stars and galaxies. The missing material is known as dark matter.

Astronomers looking at how galaxies spin around realized that dark matter must exist. The galaxies move faster than they should, and that means they are heavier than the mass of the visible stars. The rest of the galaxy is dark and invisible.

## Mystery Matter

This chart, below, shows that there is around five times more dark matter (in purple) than ordinary matter (in green). But there is also something even more mysterious called dark energy. Dark energy was discovered in 1998, and makes up around two-thirds of the energy in the Universe. It is making space expand, but physicists do not really understand it yet.

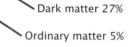

Dark matter 27%

Ordinary matter 5%

Dark energy 68%

Dark matter detectors are deep underground to shield them from all other particles and radiation.

## Detectors

Dark matter is dark because it does not produce light or any kind of radiation. Nor is it affected by electromagnetism in any way. The only force that seems to affect dark matter is gravity. The search for dark matter is very difficult and no one has found any yet. Some dark matter detectors are looking for tiny particles that might be all around us now but do not show up in standard tests.

**DID YOU KNOW?** One suggestion is that dark matter is the influence of gravity from other universes leaking into our own. No light or regular matter moves between universes, but it affects the apparent mass of matter in our universe.

Astronomers think that some dark matter might be dark objects in the halo around the edge of a galaxy.

If a galaxy was made only from the kind of regular matter that we can detect, all of its stars would be flung out into deep space as it spun around, because it wouldn't have enough mass to keep it together. Heavy dark matter inside must be pulling the galaxy together and keeping the stars in place.

**HALL OF FAME:**
Vera Rubin
1928–2016

In 1979, after studying the stars in Andromeda, the nearest big galaxy to our own, Rubin showed that dark matter makes up a lot of the mass of galaxies. She calculated the speed at which stars were moving as they went around the center of the galaxy. She found that stars at the edge were moving much too fast for the known mass of galaxy. She calculated that galaxies must have between five and ten times as much mass as we can see.

# First Law of Motion

The way objects move—how they stop, start, and change direction—is governed by three simple laws. The first law of motion is that an object will resist changing its state of motion until a force is applied to change it.

In snooker, as the cue ball collides with a red ball, it applies a force. The force alters the motion of the balls on the table. The cue ball slows down and changes direction, while the red ball starts to move.

## Adding Force

A state of motion can include being still and not going anywhere— what physicists called being at rest—or moving in a straight line at an unchanging speed. These states will carry on forever unless a force is applied. On Earth, the forces of gravity, friction, and drag will always act on a moving object to change its state of motion—and make it stop.

This car jumps as it maintains its motion and continues in a straight line—only there is no ground underneath it. The force of gravity will pull it back down.

**HALL OF FAME: Mo Di**
Fifth century BCE

Almost nothing is known about the figure referred to as Mo Di or Mozi, the author of 71 chapters of an ancient book in Chinese. He is thought to have come from a humble family and traveled around trying to persuade warlords to stop fighting one another. Much of his philosophical book has been lost, but the surviving text includes the first known statement that something will keep moving unless a force stops it—the first law of motion that Isaac Newton described in Europe 2,000 years later.

A car's body is designed to absorb the energy of a crash, so less force reaches the passenger compartment. The airbags reduce the rate at which the passengers slow to a stop.

## Inertia

The property of matter that makes it resist changes to its motion is called inertia. Inertia means it is hard to get an object moving, and once it is moving it is hard to get it to stop. In a car crash or a fall from a height, forces create a sudden change in motion—a sudden stop against a stationary object. The inertia of the moving body resists that change, and that causes injuries in a crash.

The soft and smooth green surface creates little friction, so the balls roll long distances before they stop.

Some of the force applied from the cue ball to the first red ball that the cue ball hit also applies to any other balls that red ball goes on to hit. The balls that received no force from the impact stay exactly where they are.

**DID YOU KNOW?** Force is measured in units called newtons. A force of 1 newton is enough to accelerate a mass of 1 kg (2.2 lb) by 1 m (3.3 ft) per second every.

# Second Law of Motion

The second law of motion concerns the relationship between the mass of an object, the size of the force that acts on it, and the acceleration that the force creates. The force used to move the body is calculated by multiplying the body's mass by its acceleration.

## Mass and Motion

All three features of a moving body—the mass, force, and acceleration—are proportional to one another. By increasing the force, a body will accelerate faster. When the mass of the body is increased, a larger force is needed to achieve the same acceleration. In the real world this law explains why it is easy for a person to push a bicycle along the road, but cannot easily produce the force needed to push a car in the same way.

A rescue tow truck is powerful enough to generate the force needed to move itself and the broken-down car.

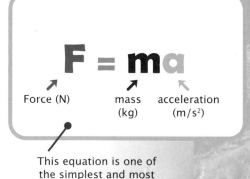

$$F = ma$$

Force (N)    mass (kg)    acceleration (m/s$^2$)

This equation is one of the simplest and most useful in physics.

## Calculating Force

The second law of motion can be defined by the simple equation: Force = mass × acceleration. This equation can be rearranged so any of the three variables can be calculated from the other two. For example, the acceleration of a body is calculated by dividing the force by the mass. The mass of the body can be calculated by dividing the force by the acceleration.

The cannon accelerates the human cannonball using a spring-loaded piston—not gunpowder!

The human cannonball is accelerated fast enough to override the pull of gravity, so the person flies through the air.

**HALL OF FAME:**
Galileo Galilei
1564–1642

This Italian scientist was one of the most important physicists of all time. He made many discoveries about the Moon and planets using his own improvements on the telescope, and carried out experiments on how objects move, especially how they fall. Galileo correctly predicted what would happen if a heavy and a lighter ball were dropped from the Leaning Tower of Pisa—that they would hit the ground at the same time.

**DID YOU KNOW?** On Earth the acceleration due to gravity is 9.8 m/s² (32 ft/s²). That means every second that gravity is applied, the object's speed increases by 9.8 m/s (32 ft/s).

# Third Law of Motion

The third law of motion is perhaps the most famous. It says that for every action there is an equal and opposite reaction. The term "action" means that a force is being applied. The "reaction" created is a force that is equal in size but pushes in the opposite direction.

It is the third law of motion that makes bumper cars so much fun. Driving into other cars gives everyone a bump!

## Rocket Engines

A rocket works by using the third law of motion. The propellants are mixed and burn with great ferocity, and the flames and gas they produce are pushed out of the bottom of the rocket. The action force caused by the rocket pushing away the gases creates a reaction force, where the gases push away the rocket. As a result, the spacecraft lifts off the ground and is powered into space.

The downward force of the exhaust gases made by the burning fuel creates an upward thrust force.

**HALL OF FAME:**
René Descartes
1596–1650

This great French philosopher is most famous for saying, "I think, therefore, I am." This was his explanation of how he knew he existed as a real person. Descartes also invented graphs and coordinates, among many other things. He came up with three laws of motion a few decades before Isaac Newton, though they were not as easy to understand as Newton's later versions.

**DID YOU KNOW?** NASA used the laws of motion to knock an asteroid off course. They simply smashed a spacecraft into it! This system will be used to make sure big asteroids do not hit Earth in the future.

## Action and Reaction

The third law explains why pushing on an object makes it move. The force of a skateboarder's foot pushing on the ground creates an opposite force of the ground pushing on the foot (and the skateboard) so the skater moves forward. To slow down, the rider pushes the skateboard tail into the ground. The ground pushes back—and the skateboard stops.

Skateboarders are using the laws of motion.

The rubber bumper stops the forces of the collisions from damaging the cars.

The mass of each car is about the same and their top speed is low, so they hit each other with a small and more or less equal force.

# Momentum

Momentum is a measure of how much motion an object has. It is calculated by multiplying the mass of an object by its velocity (speed in one direction). So a heavy truck will have more momentum than a lightweight car traveling at the same speed. The truck and the car will both have more momentum if they travel at a higher speed, and less momentum if they travel at a lower speed.

## Angular Momentum

This spinning skater makes use of momentum in a circle, called angular momentum. While she spins on the spot, she can speed up and slow down the spin in a simple way. Spreading her arms spreads out her mass, which makes her spin more slowly. Drawing in here arms pulls her mass to the middle, which makes her spin faster. Outstretched arms increase the inertia in the spin, so it slows down. Drawing the arms in decreases the inertia. The momentum stays the same, so the spin speed increases.

The point around which a skater spins is called the axis of rotation.

## Momentum Conserved

Until a new force is applied to a moving body (or a group of objects), its momentum will always stay the same. A helical spring toy is a good example of this. A small push will set the flexible spring tumbling down the stairs. At each step, the spring tips over and begins the tumbling process again because it still has momentum. It only stops at the foot of the stairs, where the force of the flat ground brings it to a halt.

This helical spring toy has very little friction interfering with its motion.

## HALL OF FAME:
### Jean Buridan
#### 1301–c.1360

This French scientist was one of the first people to come up with the idea of momentum. He called it impetus, and recognized that something could continue to move even after a force was no longer being applied to it. Buridan said that impetus could be calculated as weight × velocity. He thought that impetus was what caused motion, but now we understand that forces do that.

This set of swinging balls is called a Newton's cradle. It is a toy that shows how the momentum of a moving system is always conserved.

The moving ball will hit the next ball and transfer its momentum to it. That momentum moves through the middle balls to the farthest one, which will swing up and out.

The middle balls stay completely still while those at the ends swing back and forth. This is because all of the momentum is transferred through the middle balls to those on the ends.

**DID YOU KNOW?** Supertankers, the world biggest ships, have such a lot of momentum that it can take them 20 minutes to slow to a stop!

# Velocity and Acceleration

When measuring motion, physicists use three basic measurements—time, distance, and direction. Together, these can be used to calculate velocity, which is the distance traveled over time in a certain direction. When forces are applied, they create acceleration. Acceleration is a change in the velocity, increasing or decreasing it.

A dragster's enormous engine is designed to push the car forward with as much force as possible. The car will be accelerating throughout the whole race.

## The Need for Speed

Speed is a simple measure of how fast an object is moving. Velocity is a speed in a particular direction. Objects traveling at the same speed but in different directions have different velocities. This is especially important when they are traveling toward each other. If their speed is the same, the relative velocity (how fast one is moving in relation to the other) will be twice the individual object's speed.

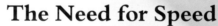

This runner's speed is calculated by measuring the time it takes for him to move a known distance.

**HALL OF FAME:**
Katherine Johnson
1918–2020

Johnson was a mathematician working at NASA when the first rockets were being launched into space. It was her job to calculate the flightpaths that rockets took as they flew up into orbit. John Glenn, the first American astronaut to orbit Earth, asked Johnson before his flight to check the velocity calculations made by the computer. When she said they were correct, Glenn was happy to launch.

**DID YOU KNOW?** The fastest speed in the universe is the speed of light through a vacuum. That is 300,000 km per second (186,000 mi per second).

A drag race runs along a straight course. The winning car is the one that can accelerate fastest.

Making the car so long helps it stay on the ground as it zooms along.

Steering around a bend is a form of acceleration.

## Changing Speed

Acceleration occurs when a force is applied to move an object. It is a measure of the rate of change of velocity. Acceleration is expressed as how much the speed will increase or decrease every second that the force is being applied. When the force stops, the acceleration also stops and the velocity remains constant. A force may keep the speed unchanged but change the direction of the object—and thus change its velocity. This is also acceleration.

# Oscillation

Some moving systems move back and forth around a central point, in a motion called oscillation. This happens because a restoring force is always pulling the moving object back to the central position. Oscillating bodies repeat the same motion over and over again, always moving the same distances and taking the same time.

## Pendulums

The most familiar oscillators are pendulums, which are a weight, called the bob, on a string or rod. The bob swings from side to side. The period, or time it takes to complete each swing, depends on the length of the rod. Gravity is the restoring force. At the end of the swing, gravity has slowed the bob to a stop, but then pulls it back so that it swings to the middle again. Its momentum keeps moving it to the other side. The process then repeats.

Bouncing on a trampoline makes a person act as an oscillator. The bouncy surface pushes them upward and then gravity slows that rise and makes them fall again.

The pendulum's bob reaches top speed as it passes through the central point.

## HALL OF FAME: Christiaan Huygens
### 1629–1695

This Dutch scientist and inventor made the first pendulum clock in 1657. He used the regular swing of a pendulum to keep time. The motion of the pendulum turns the minute and hour hands. As well as his work with clocks, Huygens was also the first to suggest that Saturn was surrounded by rings.

## Restoring Force

Springs are good oscillators that bounce up and down when a weight is attached underneath, stretching the spring out of shape. The restoring force is the spring pulling or pushing itself back into its original shape. How much a weight stretches a spring (or a rope) obeys Hooke's Law. This law says that the amount of stretch (and the restoring force) is proportional to the weight. If you double the weight, the stretch also doubles.

Instead of stretching it, too much weight will eventually deform and break the spring.

The trampoliner can increase the height and period of each bounce by adding an extra push.

**DID YOU KNOW?** For a pendulum to pass through the center of its swing once a second, it needs to be 99 cm (39 inches) long.

37

# Rotational Motion

Rotational motion is produced when objects spin or move around in circles. While in rotational motion, the object's velocity is always changing as it traces a circular path. A force pulling the object to the middle of the circle causes this constant change of direction.

## Centrifugal Force

Centrifugal force is sometimes mentioned as one form of rotational motion. It refers to the tendency of a rotating object to fly away from the middle of the circle. But there is not really such a force. The object's inertia drives it to travel in a straight line—which happens to take it away from the middle. If another force pulls the object to the middle, the result is circular motion. When a wet dog shakes its fur, the water is flung away by the centrifugal force.

A wet dog rotates its body back and forth to throw the water sideways.

## HALL OF FAME: Robert Hooke
### 1635–1703

This British scientist is famous for Hooke's law of elasticity—how weights stretch materials—which he discovered in the seventeenth century. Hooke was one of the most prolific scientists of his day and worked on gravity, clocks, microscopes, and many other things. Professional disputes led to him being overshadowed by Isaac Newton and Christiaan Huygens.

# Centripetal Force

A centripetal force pulls an object toward the middle of a circle. This works against the inertia that would make it move in a straight line, with the result that the object moves in a circle. If you swing a ball on a string, the centripetal force is provided by the string. When Earth moves around the Sun, the Sun's gravity is the centripetal force.

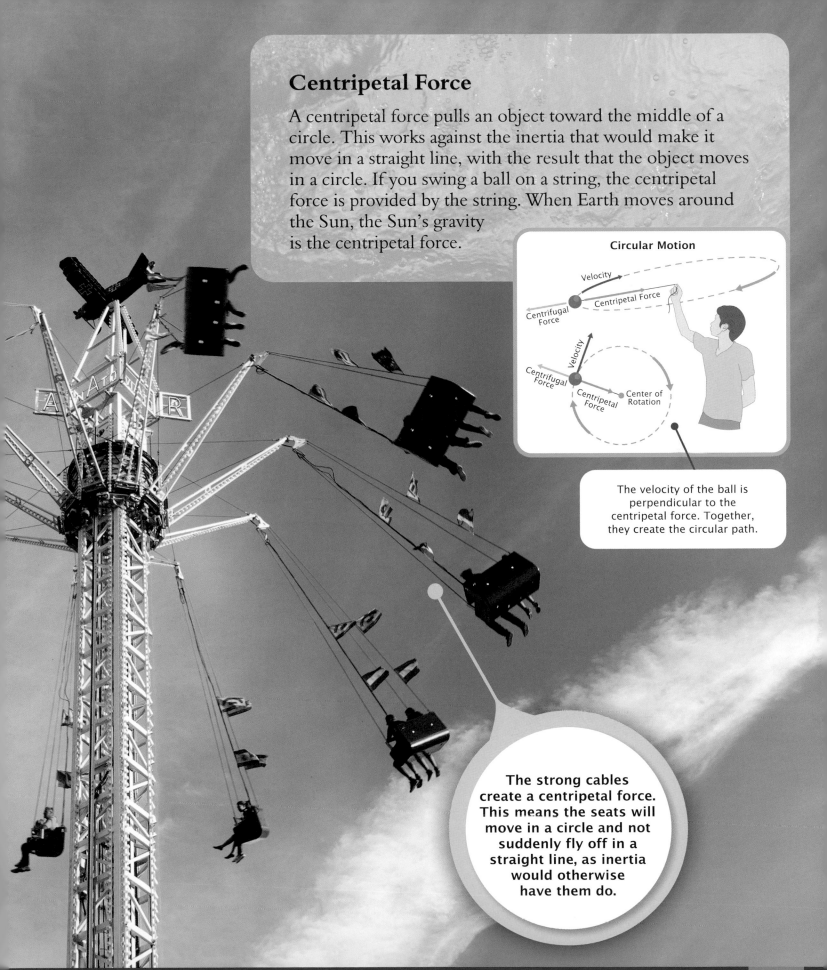

**Circular Motion**

Velocity

Centripetal Force

Centrifugal Force

Velocity

Centrifugal Force

Centripetal Force

Center of Rotation

The velocity of the ball is perpendicular to the centripetal force. Together, they create the circular path.

The strong cables create a centripetal force. This means the seats will move in a circle and not suddenly fly off in a straight line, as inertia would otherwise have them do.

**DID YOU KNOW?** The fastest natural rotations on Earth are within whirlwinds or tornadoes. The air inside can move at 500 km/h (300 mph).

39

# Orbits and Weightlessness

An orbit is the path a small body follows around a larger one. It is most familiar in astronomy—planets orbit the Sun and moons orbit planets. The gravity of the larger body holds the smaller body in its orbit. Artificial satellites and space stations orbit Earth using the same forces. Very small objects in orbit—including people—appear to be weightless.

## A Sense of Motion

An orbit is a very special kind of falling. The gravity of a planet or star provides the centripetal force that pulls a body, such as a moon, planet, or satellite, toward it. On its own, this would make the body fall. But the inertia of the orbiting body means it keeps trying to move away. Both together produce rotational movement. The object doesn't complete its fall but is said to be in free fall—when the only force acting on an object is gravity.). An orbiting satellite, including any astronauts inside, seems to float, as if weightless.

Astronauts in orbit are in free fall, just like this skydiver, only they will never reach the ground!

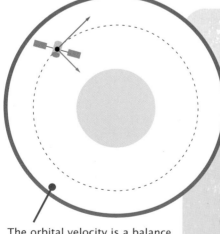

The orbital velocity is a balance between the pull of gravity and the satellite's inertia that is flinging it out into space.

## Orbital Velocity

The height of an orbit is called its altitude. The orbital velocity—the speed at which the object moves around the planet—depends on its altitude. A satellite orbiting near to Earth must move much faster than one that is in orbit farther away from Earth. If the satellite slows down, gravity will overcome inertia and pull the satellite down to Earth.

**DID YOU KNOW?** The International Space Station orbits 400 km (250 miles) above the surface of Earth.

It is not a lack of gravity that makes astronauts seem weightless. Gravity in Earth's orbit is only very slightly weaker than at Earth's surface.

There is no up or down in orbit, and the human body finds it hard to regulate itself without an obvious pull of gravity. Being weightless slowly damages the body.

The astronauts and spacecraft float in space but they still have mass and momentum. To be moved around, they still require the same forces as on Earth.

**HALL OF FAME:**
Johannes Kepler
1571–1630

This German astronomer discovered the relationship between motion and orbits by studying how planets move through the sky. Kepler discovered that planets do not have circular orbits, but move around the Sun in elliptical (squashed circle) orbits. That means their distance from the Sun constantly changes. Planets move more quickly when they're closest to the Sun and more slowly when they're farther away.

# Ballistics

The study of how objects move as they are thrown or shot through the air is called ballistics. This kind of motion has two components. The force of the throw accelerates the object forward (and possibly upward), while the force of gravity pulls the object back down again. Ballistics analyzes these forces to figure out where the object will land.

The javelin thrower must get the angle just right to ensure the force of his throw will make the spear fly a long horizontal distance. The best angle is 45 degrees.

## Curved Path

The interaction between the force of the throw—or a gunshot or rocket boost—and the force of gravity makes a thrown object trace a curved path through the air. The type of curve is called a parabola, where the rising path and the falling path match. The parabola has a vertical height and a horizontal width. The size of these measurements depends on the size of the force of the throw and its angle.

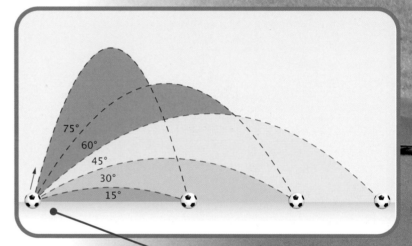

75°
60°
45°
30°
15°

Kicking at a lower angle makes a flatter, wider curve. But if the curve is too flat, gravity will pull the object down sooner than something traveling at a higher angle.

## Beating Gravity

Ballistics can also be used to figure out how to launch spacecraft. If a rocket engine provides enough force, the rocket will be able to reach orbital velocity, when its speed is enough to balance the pull of gravity. Instead of falling back down to Earth, the rocket will follow a path around the planet.

If the rocket pushes even more, the spacecraft will eventually achieve escape velocity and fly away from Earth completely.

This Italian mathematician and engineer was the first person to apply mathematics to the study of ballistics, working out the trajectories of cannonballs. He discovered that firing a cannonball at an angle of 45 degrees gave it the longest reach. He was also the first person to translate the hugely important mathematical works of the ancient Greek mathematician Euclid into a modern European language.

The thrower will rock his body forward as he swings the javelin overhead. This transfers all of his weight to the javelin, sending it on its way with great force.

The skill of the thrower is to apply a force that makes the javelin fly straight into its parabola. It is all too easy for the javelin to twist and flip in the air.

**DID YOU KNOW?** The longest throw of an object without wings or a tail was a boomerang thrown by David Schummy in 2005. It went 427.2 m (1,401.5 ft).

# Flight

Flying through the air is difficult, and it involves four forces. The downward pull of gravity is counteracted by an upward lift. A thrust force pushes forward while the air resistance or drag pushes back. To fly through the air, lift must balance gravity, and thrust must outweigh drag.

The upright tail of an aircraft is there to stop it from rolling over to one side. A rudder can be used to steer the plane from side to side.

## Lift Force

An aircraft's wing is designed to produce lift. The wing has a particular curved shape, called an airfoil or aerofoil, which makes air flowing over it move faster than air flowing beneath it. The slower air is more bunched up, so it has a higher pressure than the faster air. The high-pressure air pushes the wing up, creating lift. For the wing to work like this, the thrust force must push it through the air very fast.

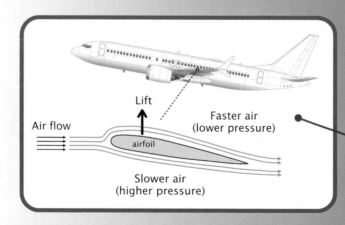

Lift

Air flow

airfoil

Faster air (lower pressure)

Slower air (higher pressure)

Only once the lift force is greater than gravity will the aircraft take off into the air.

## HALL OF FAME: Daniel Bernoulli 1700–1782

The way in which a wing creates lift is called the Bernoulli Effect. It is named for the Swiss mathematician who developed ways of calculating how air and water move. Bernoulli was also interested in the mathematics of chance and statistics, which is a way of showing if something is true or false, or likely or unlikely, using data.

Computer models help show how air moves around an aircraft as it flies.

## Aerodynamics

Planes travel through the air at hundreds of miles an hour. At that speed, the drag force created by air resistance will have a big effcct. Aircraft designers need to understand aerodynamics, which is how air flows around the aircraft. Smooth, sleek shapes create less drag.

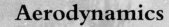

Everything that flies, from planes and birds to helicopters, makes use of the same forces.

The wings of an aircraft have moving parts called flaps and ailerons. They change the shape of the wing to create more lift or to make the plane change direction.

**DID YOU KNOW?** The rocket-powered X–15 holds the record for the fastest piloted aircraft, with a top speed of 7,274 km/h (4,520 mph).

# Buoyancy

How is it that a ship weighing many thousands of tonnes can float in water, while a coin weighing very little will sink to the bottom? Understanding buoyancy, or how things float, begins with density. Density is a measure of how much mass is contained in an object. A bucket of water is heavier than a bucket of air, because water is denser than air. Anything denser than water will sink, while everything else floats in it.

## Pushing Back

Wood is less dense than water so it floats, while a metal weight is much denser so it sinks. When a solid falls in water, gravity pulls it down. Meanwhile the water around the object pushes back creating an upward buoyant force. When the object is denser than water, gravity beats the buoyant force and the object sinks. If the object is less dense than water, the buoyant force will counteract gravity, so the object floats.

The strength of the buoyant force is equal to the weight of the water pushed aside by the object as it sits in the water.

Weight
Object
Fluid
Buoyant force

This metal ship is one of the largest and heaviest things ever built. However, its huge size is not important. It floats because it is less dense than water.

## Floating in Air

Balloons and airships fly by floating in the air. An aircraft like this is less dense than the air itself. The buoyant force of the gases all around it is stronger than the pull of gravity—and the balloon floats up into the air! Airships are filled with helium, a very lightweight gas, while hot-air balloons become lighter by heating the air inside.

The air inside these giant balloons is spread out by being heated so it has a lower density to the colder air on the outside.

The density of sea water depends on its temperature and its saltiness. Fresh water is less dense than salty water. All ships have a load line painted on their hull that shows how much cargo the vessel can safely carry in different conditions.

This ship is big! On land each one of these rectangular containers has to be pulled along by their own truck.

## HALL OF FAME:
Cornelis Drebbel
1572-1633

This Dutch engineer invented the world's first submarine in 1620. His craft looked like a large boat-shaped barrel. Drebbel was able to control its buoyancy with air pumps so it sank underwater and then floated back up to the surface. William Shakespeare heard about this and Drebbel's other inventions. He was inspired to write The Tempest, a play about a wizard-like scientist.

**DID YOU KNOW?** Ice is the only solid that floats in its liquid form—water. Other substances grow denser as they freeze.

# Doing Work

To a physicist, the term "work" has a very particular meaning: Work is the transfer of energy from one object to another. Work can only happen when a force is applied. Work is measured using units of energy called joules.

In its simplest form, work is using a force to move a mass over a distance. Lifting these sacks is hard work!

## Heating Up

When work is done, some of the energy being transferred will become heat. That heat energy is no longer usable and leaks away from the system. This leaking of energy is due to a process called entropy, which means energy tends to spread out. As a result, any working system, from a machine to your body, will always lose energy and eventually stop working unless more force is applied.

Exercise makes us hot because our muscles warm up as they work hard.

## Falling Down

The water in this waterfall is doing work as it gushes downward. At the top, the water has potential energy. This is energy it has as a result of its position or state, which can be converted to another form. When gravity causes the water to fall over the cliff, the water's potential energy is converted into kinetic (motion) energy.

The water is a little bit hotter at the bottom of the waterfall because some of the kinetic energy is converted into heat energy.

48

The unit of energy, the joule, is named after this British scientist. He wanted to show that heat and motion are related kinds of energy. In the 1860s Joule performed a famous experiment where he used a falling weight to spin a stirrer in a tank of water. He showed that dropping the weight over and over again made the water gradually get warmer.

The unit of energy, the joule (J), is calculated by multiplying force by distance. So 1 J is the work done when 1 kg (2.2 lb) is moved 1 m (3.2 ft) in 1 second.

The energy from the muscles is transferred to the sack, so it moves up from the ground to the back of the truck.

**DID YOU KNOW?** The average human body uses about 10 million joules in 24 hours.

# Thermal Energy

Physicists call heat energy "thermal energy." It is held by the atoms and molecules in a substance. As the atoms gain thermal energy, they vibrate faster, and the material becomes hotter. Thermal energy is always on the move. It spreads out from hot things to colder things until eventually everything is the same temperature.

The metalworker wears thick, insulated gloves that prevent the heat passing through and burning the skin.

## Heat Transfer

There are three ways thermal energy moves—conduction, convection, and radiation. Conduction happens in solids as atoms jostle one another. Convection is caused by warm liquids and gases rising up through colder ones. As hot material cools and falls again, it is replaced by newly heated matter rising, setting up a current that spreads heat. Radiation carries the energy as invisible heat rays, called infrared waves.

Conduction

Convection

Radiation

As the warm water rises, it begins to cool and then sinks. This creates a circular current that moves the heat around.

Temperature scales fix an upper and lower point and divide the gap between into units called degrees. This thermometer shows that the temperature is at the freezing point of water.

°C °F

## Taking the Temperature

Temperature is a measure of the average kinetic energy of the particles in a substance. Temperature is not a measure of the total energy in the material. An iceberg, for example, contains many more atoms than a hot spark coming from a fire, so it carries much more energy in total. However, the spark is at a much higher temperature. Thermometers are used to measure temperature.

Heat is passing along the red-hot iron by conduction. The hot atoms hit their colder neighbors, making them move around more—and become hotter.

An expert can tell the temperature of the metal from the color of its glow.

**HALL OF FAME:**
Lord Kelvin
1824–1907

Born William Thomson, this Irish physicist worked on heat and other forms of energy. He not only transformed the understanding of physics but also helped create new technologies, such as refrigeration and telecommunications. Kelvin discovered that the minimum possible temperature, or absolute zero, is –273°C (–459°F). This is the temperature at which matter has the smallest possible amount of thermal energy. It is now known as 0 Kelvins, with each Kelvin equivalent to 1°C.

**DID YOU KNOW?** Half the energy from the Sun is invisible infrared heat waves. Light makes up two-fifths of the Sun's energy that reaches the surface of Earth.

# Kinetic Energy

The energy of motion is called kinetic energy. Kinetic energy is most obvious when it is making big things like cars and trains move. The Moon, Earth, Sun—and all other objects in the Universe—are moving as well. Even at the smallest scale, moving atoms have kinetic energy.

## Speed and Safety

As an object's velocity increases, so does its kinetic energy—but not by the same amount. When speed doubles, the kinetic energy increases by four times. So to go at twice the speed an object needs four times as much energy. This is why speed limits on roads are important. Even small increases in speed mean that vehicles are moving with much more energy and can do more damage in a collision.

The speed limits for heavy vehicles like trucks are lower than for cars because trucks carry more kinetic energy and would be more dangerous in an accident.

## Energy Transfer

When one moving object collides with another, the faster object transfers kinetic energy to the slower one. As well as being linked to velocity, the kinetic energy is proportional to the mass of the moving body. So if two objects are moving at the same speed, the larger one always has more energy. How much energy is transferred in collisions depends on the angle of the collision and how hard or flexible the objects are.

The tackler absorbs the kinetic energy of his opponent, stopping him.

The wheels on a road–racing bike are able to grip the road so no energy is lost to slipping. The wheels get hot as they turn fast.

Bicycles are the most efficient means of transport. They convert more of the energy applied into kinetic energy than other vehicles.

## HALL OF FAME: Émilie du Châtelet
### 1706–1749

This French scientist and mathematician linked the idea of kinetic energy to mass and velocity. She also helped to explain that energy of any kind is never made or destroyed, but transformed into other types. Much of du Châtelet's work is found in her translation of Isaac Newton's writings, to which she added her own ideas and improvements.

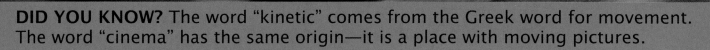

**DID YOU KNOW?** The word "kinetic" comes from the Greek word for movement. The word "cinema" has the same origin—it is a place with moving pictures.

# Potential Energy

While kinetic energy is concerned with motion of all kinds, potential energy is how energy can be stored by objects in different ways. This energy is transferred to objects when work (see page 48) is done to them. The energy is always there, even when the object seems to be doing nothing—and it can be released when the conditions are right.

The riders on the rollercoaster feel the sudden release of gravitational potential energy. After being lifted slowly to the top of a hill, they then roll down the other side under the pull of gravity.

## Electrical Potential

One form of potential energy is electrical potential energy. This is the energy stored in batteries. It is created whenever a difference in electrical charge is created, where positive charges and negative charges are kept separated. To rebalance that charge and release the electrical potential energy, electrons move as an electric current (a form of kinetic energy).

To recharge a battery, an electric current is used to push charged particles apart to create a store of potential energy. When the battery is used, that potential is released.

## Elastic Potential

Some solid materials will deform (change shape) when a force is applied to them. Permanent changes are called plastic deformations. Energy is not stored in the new shape. Temporary changes are called elastic deformations, and the shape will spring back to normal when the force is released. The energy stored in the stretched material is elastic potential energy. This kind of energy makes balls bounce and is used in spring-loaded and wind-up devices.

Adding elastic potential energy to this bungee helps to work the muscles and keep them strong.

**DID YOU KNOW?** Rivers flow due to the water's gravitational potential energy. Rain falls high on mountains and the water is pulled back to the ocean by gravity.

It takes a lot of work to push the rollercoaster up to this point. That work is converted into gravitational potential energy, which is released as the cars roll down the other side.

Gravity is making the cars accelerate at a similar speed to if they were in free fall through the air. The curved track will then slow the cars down gradually.

# Other Types of Energy

One of the main laws of physics is the conservation of energy. This law says that energy is never created or destroyed. Instead, it is transformed from one type of energy into another. As well as motion, heat, and potential energy, there are several other kinds of energy.

## Electrical Energy

Most modern machines are powered using electrical energy. This is a flow of energy that is carried by a current of electrons. A very simple electrical machine is a heater, where the flow of electrons pushes on atoms in a wire, converting their electrical energy to heat (and perhaps visible light, too). Electric motors use magnets to create forces that make moving parts spin.

The microchips inside a computer are powered by electricity. They use the energy to perform calculations and follow instructions. The computer screen is also lit by electricity.

## Sound Energy

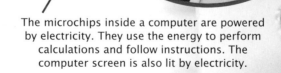

Sound is a wave of pressure that moves through the air. It is a kind of kinetic energy because the sound wave is moving the air molecules, causing them to spread apart and then squeeze together. Sound waves are created by kinetic energy from other materials being transferred to the air. Loud sounds contain more energy than quiet ones.

A megaphone has a cone that wobbles back and forth very fast. That wobble creates a sound wave—a loud one!

Energy is released when bonds between atoms break. Some of that free energy is then used to rearrange the atoms into new substances.

Chemical reactions involve chemical energy. The energy is stored in the links or bonds between atoms. This is a kind of potential energy.

If any energy is left over it is often released as heat or light.

**HALL OF FAME:**
Laura Bassi
1711–1778

Born in what is now Bologna, Italy, Bassi became only the second woman in the world to earn a PhD, or doctorate. She was also the first woman to have a paid job as a teacher at Bologna's university, where she taught physics. Bassi studied electricity and became the main researcher in the physics department at the university.

**DID YOU KNOW?** Thinking uses energy. Your brain uses up 20 percent of the energy your body needs each day.

# Power

Work is a measure of the transfer of energy from one object to another. Power is a measure of how quickly the energy is transferred. For example, it takes the same amount of work for two swimmers of the same mass to swim a length of a pool, but a more powerful swimmer can do that work in less time.

This immensely powerful truck can move a very large load in a short amount of time.

## Watts

Power is measured in units called watts (W), named after James Watt. He used the idea of power to explain why his steam-powered inventions were able to work better than human workers. One watt (1 W) is 1 joule (1 J) of energy transferred in a second. Most of our appliances at home have a power rating expressed in watts. This tells us how much energy they will use up. A machine with a lower power rating saves energy but might take longer to do the job.

The brightness of light bulbs is measured in watts. Floodlights are around 10,000 times more powerful than the lights in your home.

**HALL OF FAME:** James Watt 1736-1809

This Scottish engineer is known for his work on the steam engine. He improved on earlier designs to create machines that were efficient to use. Before Watt, steam engines used a lot of fuel but were not very powerful. Watt's engines were large and powerful and were meant to be used in factories and mines. Later inventors made smaller engines for ships and trains.

This truck is a complex machine that uses several kinds of simpler machines, such as wheels, levers, and pulleys, to do work efficiently.

## Using Power

A machine can be more powerful than a human body. This means one machine can do the work of many people. The original unit of power was horsepower. Early machines were compared to the strength and power of horses, which were used to haul heavy loads. The power of cars and other vehicles is sometimes still measured in horsepower today. One horsepower is about 740 W, and it is estimated that one horse can exert 10 times as much power as a person.

This forklift can lift more weight than a person and it can do it faster and go higher, too.

The dump truck uses powerful pistons to push up the load so that it slides off the back.

**DID YOU KNOW?** The most powerful rocket engine ever built, the F–1 that launched NASA's Saturn V Moon rockets, had a power rating of 41 million watts.

59

# Levers

There are six types of simple machines that are often combined in mechanisms. A machine is any system that carries out work, converting an effort (a force applied by user) into a load (a force applied by machine, e.g. a lever). To be useful, a machine reduces the effort needed to do something. This is called providing a mechanical advantage. The simplest machine is a lever.

## Three Classes of Lever

A lever is a stiff rod that moves around a fulcrum—the turning or balancing point. A first-class lever, such as a seesaw, has the fulcrum in the middle, with the effort and load forces on either side. Pushing one side down (effort) makes the other side go up (load). A second-class lever, like a wheelbarrow, has the fulcrum at one end and the effort at the other. The load is applied in the middle. Tweezers are third-class levers, where the effort force is applied between the fulcrum and the load at both ends.

This wheelbarrow is a second–class lever. The gardener's effort lifts the handles. The lever turns at the wheel, and the load in the barrow is held in the middle.

Scissors are a pair of first–class levers connected at the fulcrum. Each lever has a cutting edge that slides past the other.

## Changing Forces

A lever is a force multiplier, which means the size of the effort and the load forces are different. A lever can't change the work done to be greater than the effort, but it can exert a larger force over a shorter distance. This is what happens when you use a lever to lift something heavy. You could not move the large object directly, but by moving one end of a lever a long distance you can convert the effort into enough energy to move the object a small distance at the other end.

The rowers pull the handle forward and the oar blade at the other end moves backward through the water. The effort force on the handle is translated into a load that pushes the boat along.

The effort force is applied nearer to the fulcrum than the load force, and so moves the lever a smaller distance. The effort needed to move a load is related to the distance of the force from the fulcrum.

**HALL OF FAME:**
Archimedes
287–212 BCE

This great ancient Greek mathematician lived in what is now Sicily. As well as making mathematical discoveries, Archimedes also made several inventions, mostly to defend his city from attacks by the Romans. One of these inventions was a lever system that could hook onto a ship and unbalance it so that it sank.

**DID YOU KNOW?** The oldest known lever-based machine was a balance scale used for weighing objects. It was made in Mesopotamia (now Iraq) around 7,000 years ago.

# Ramps and Screws

Other simple machines are ramps, wedges, and screws, all of which share the same feature of have a thin end and getting wider along their length. A ramp (or inclined plane) makes it easier to lift heavy objects, a wedge is a cutting machine, and a screw is a mixture of both.

This screw-shaped machine is called an auger. It is twisted into the ground to dig a hole.

## Inclined Plane

Work is calculated as force × distance. Lifting a heavy load straight up in one go requires a large force to be applied for short time. A ramp makes it possible for the same amount of work to be done using a smaller force over a longer distance. A flight of stairs is a kind of ramp. It would be very hard work to move between floors without stairs!

The giant stone slabs of the pyramids of Egypt were probably lifted into place using ramps.

## Cutting Edge

A wedge has the same basic shape as an inclined plane, with a thin end and a thick end. The wedge is a force multiplier. When an effort force is applied to the thicker side, that force is concentrated in the thin end, which is often a sharp blade. The concentration of force creates very high pressure, so the wedge can cut through what it touches.

An ax head has a wedge shape that slices through most things.

**DID YOU KNOW?** The first ever machine was the Stone-Age hand ax, a wedge-shaped cutter that was invented by our prehuman ancestors more than a million years ago!

Van Schurman is best remembered as a poet and artist but she was also the first woman to go to university in Europe. She was highly intelligent and was able to speak at least 14 languages! This allowed Van Schurman to exchange letters with many important people all over Europe. The letters discussed all kinds of things, including the latest ideas in physics. Van Schurman helped many people, women and men, learn new things about the world.

The screw works like a wedge or ramp wrapped around in a spiral. As the screw turns, it cuts into the ground and lifts the loose soil up and out of the hole.

Another name for an auger is an Archimedes screw. As well as digging holes, it can be used to lift water and powders.

# Wheels and Pulleys

The wheel is a very famous machine. It was probably first used about 5,500 years ago for making pottery. Only later was it repurposed to move carts and wagons. A pulley is a hoist system that uses several wheels together to make it easier to lift heavy loads.

## Mechanical Advantage

The simplest types of pulleys use a single wheel with a rope looped around it. This machine just reverses the direction of a force. If you pull down on one side of the rope— the effort force—the other side pulls up with a load force of the same size. A compound pulley with more than one wheel acts as a force multiplier. A pulley with two wheels can move a load four times greater than the effort. However, the compound pulley must be pulled four times as far for it to lift a load to the same height as the simple pulley.

This movable pulley is used to lift and raise loads attached to the hook.

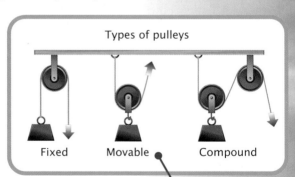

Types of pulleys

Fixed          Movable          Compound

A pulley shares the weight of the load between both sides of the rope, and so less effort is needed to lift it.

**HALL OF FAME:**
al-Jazari
1136–1206

This Arab engineer and inventor is best remembered for building life-like automata. An automaton is a simple kind of robot that can only perform a limited set of movements. Al-Jazari used pulleys and other machines powered by waterwheels to make automata that poured drinks or played music.

The spokes of the wheel spread out from the axle to keep the rim rigid, but make the wheel lighter than if it were a solid disk.

## Axle Needed

Vehicles need wheels to move. A wheel rotates around an axle, which is a stiff rod attached to the middle of the wheel and connected to the vehicle. In most cases, the wheel turns because rotational motion is transferred to it via the axle. For each rotation of the axle, the wheel turns once. The vehicle moves a distance along the road equal to the distance around the rim of the wheel, which is much longer than the distance around the axle.

The compound pulley here is attached to cables that can raise and lower the crane's long boom, or arm.

This large pedestal crane is used to lift loads in and out of a ship's hold.

**DID YOU KNOW?** The largest wheel was a pleasure ride in Dubai. At 250 m (820 ft) across, it was more than twice the length of a football field.

# Engines

An engine is a complex machine that harnesses the heat energy released by a burning fuel. It can be used to drive a vehicle over land or water, or through the air or space. Most engines burn fossil fuels and that creates dangerous pollution. In future, many engines will be replaced by electric motors.

A jet engine burns a hot mixture of air and fuel. The gases made by the burning produce a jet that blasts out the back, creating a thrust force.

## Heat Engines

The simplest engines are external combustion engines. The fuel is burned outside the engine, and its energy is transferred to it by a working fluid, which pushes on the moving parts of the engine to create motion. The best example is a steam engine. The working fluid is water that is boiled into steam. In an internal combustion engine, like those in cars, ships, and planes, the fuel itself is the working fluid.

Steam engines are very inefficient and dirty. They have not been used for many years.

## Gears

The motion of the engine is transmitted to the wheels of a car or a ship's propeller via a series of gears. The gears are interlocking wheels. When one turns, the gears touching it will also move, only they turn in the opposite direction. The number of turns the gears make depends on the number of interlocking teeth. If an adjoining gear has half as many teeth as the main wheel, it will turn at twice the speed.

Gears are used to manage the forces coming from the engine.

The jet engine works by converting chemical energy into the kinetic energy of fast-moving gases.

The flow of gas also drives fan-like turbines that draw in more air and squeeze it to boost the burning process.

**DID YOU KNOW?** The first engine was the aeolipile invented by Hero of Alexandria 2,000 years ago. It was a simple steam engine that spun around powered by jets of hot steam.

# Properties of a Wave

> Waves have high peaks and low troughs. The wavelength is the distance from one peak to the next.

Many forms of energy travel as waves. A wave is a vibration that transfers energy from one place to another without transferring matter. All waves have wavelength, frequency, and amplitude. Although light and sound are very different, because they are both waves they behave in predictable ways. The properties of a wave determine how it appears to us—as a high sound or a red light, for example.

## Frequency

The frequency of a wave is how many complete oscillations, or cycles, the wave makes every second. Frequency is measured in hertz (Hz), and a wave with a frequency of 1 Hz completes one oscillation in one second. Frequency is a good indication of the energy in a wave. High-frequency waves carry more energy than low-frequency waves of the same type.

These instruments make sound waves with different frequencies. Our ears detect high-frequency sounds as high-pitched notes, while low-frequency notes sound deeper.

## HALL OF FAME: Pythagoras
c.570–c495 BCE

This ancient Greek mathematician is most famous for his work on right-angle triangles. However, among many other discoveries, Pythagoras found a link between the note made by a string on a musical instrument and the string's length. Halving the length of the string moves the note up one octave.

## Speed

A wave's speed is calculated by multiplying its wavelength by its frequency—so if the wavelength is 0.5 m (1.6 ft) and the frequency is 5 Hz, the speed is 0.5 × 5 = 2.5 m per second (or 1.6 x 5 = 8.2 ft per second). Sound waves and ocean waves can travel at different speeds, but the speed of light is always the same when it travels through the same medium. It is fastest in the vacuum of space, and slows down slightly in air and even more in water.

This jet fighter is punching through the sound barrier, creating a puff of cloud as it moves faster through the air than sound waves can.

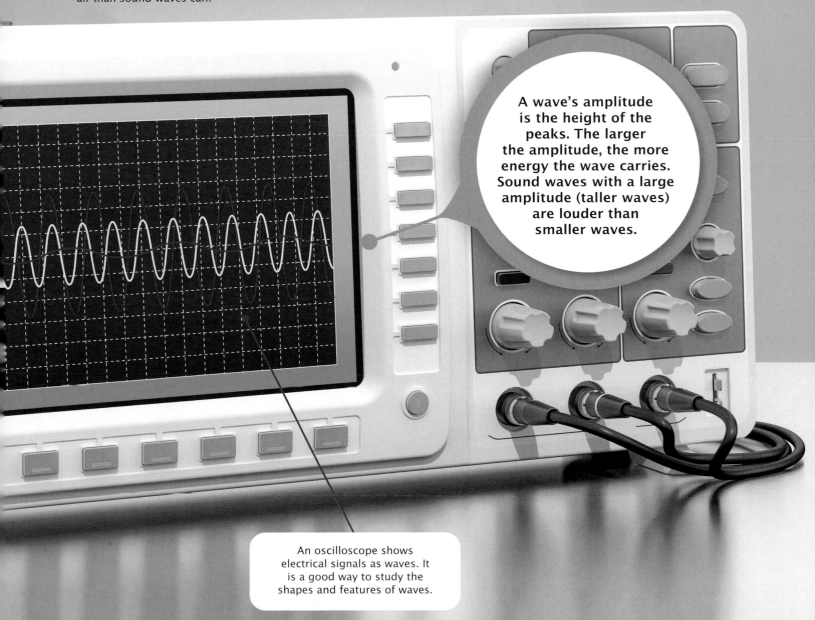

A wave's amplitude is the height of the peaks. The larger the amplitude, the more energy the wave carries. Sound waves with a large amplitude (taller waves) are louder than smaller waves.

An oscilloscope shows electrical signals as waves. It is a good way to study the shapes and features of waves.

**DID YOU KNOW?** Earthquakes are caused by powerful seismic waves that ripple through Earth. When they reach the surface, the waves make the ground shake.

# Types of Waves

A wave is the form energy takes when traveling. There are three kinds of waves—Longitudinal, transverse, and surface waves. Each one oscillates in a particular way. Sound waves and some seismic waves (the waves that run through Earth's interior) are longitudinal. Light and other radiation are transverse waves, while the swells of an ocean are surface waves.

Longitudinal waves, such as sound, need a medium to travel through, such as air. There is no sound in space because it is empty—there is no medium.

## Surface Waves

A surface wave forms where two substances meet. The most familiar are the waves in the sea, where water and air meet at the surface. The water itself does not move with the wave. Instead, the wave's peaks and troughs form as water moves up and down, cycling in the same place.

Ocean waves break in shallow water because the bottom section of the wave slows as it drags along the seabed and the top half topples forward.

A loudspeaker converts an electrical signal coming from the guitar into a vibration that creates a sound wave in the air. That wave matches the sound made by the guitar—only it is much louder!

**HALL OF FAME:**
Inge Lehmann
1888–1993

This Danish scientist was a pioneer of seismology, the study of waves moving underground. Lehmann discovered Earth's solid inner core in 1936. She investigated powerful waves made by earthquakes on the other side of the world. These waves traveled through the middle of the planet, and the way some were blocked or reflected revealed to Lehmann that Earth's hot metal core has an inner region made from solid metal.

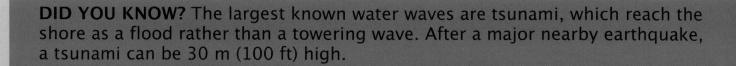

**DID YOU KNOW?** The largest known water waves are tsunami, which reach the shore as a flood rather than a towering wave. After a major nearby earthquake, a tsunami can be 30 m (100 ft) high.

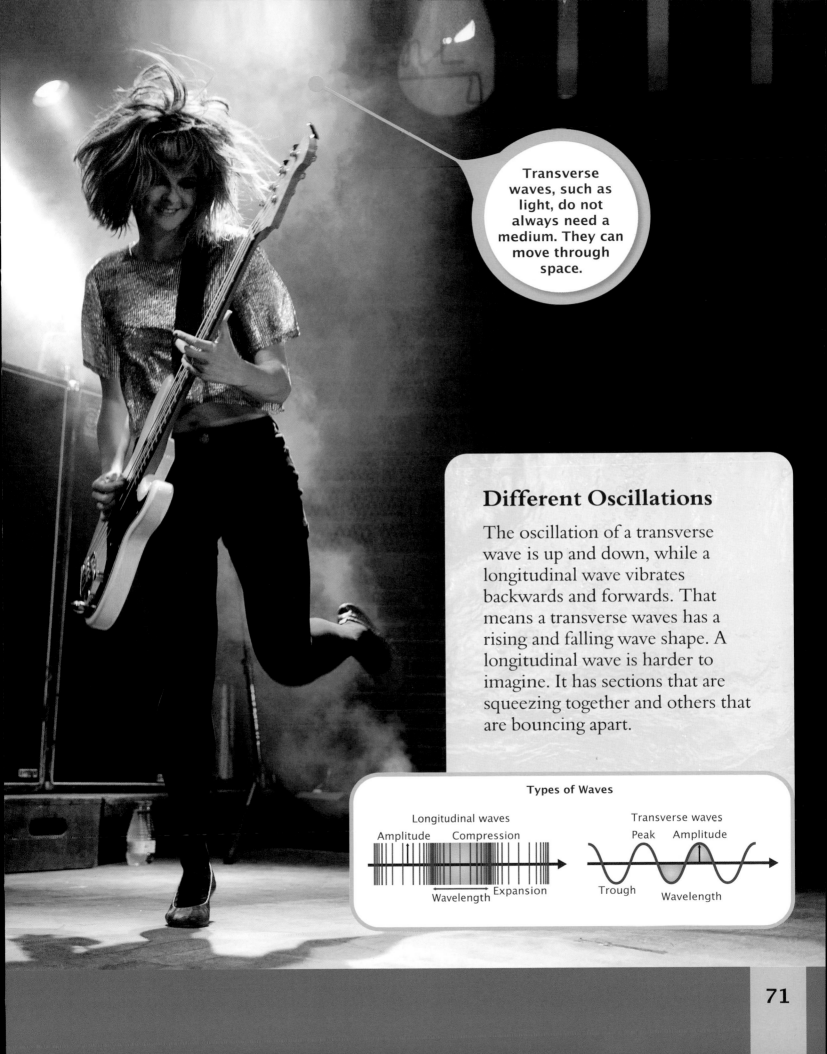

Transverse waves, such as light, do not always need a medium. They can move through space.

## Different Oscillations

The oscillation of a transverse wave is up and down, while a longitudinal wave vibrates backwards and forwards. That means a transverse waves has a rising and falling wave shape. A longitudinal wave is harder to imagine. It has sections that are squeezing together and others that are bouncing apart.

**Types of Waves**

Longitudinal waves

Amplitude    Compression

Wavelength    Expansion

Transverse waves

Peak    Amplitude

Trough    Wavelength

# Electromagnetic Spectrum

Light waves are just one part of a wider range of waves called the electromagnetic spectrum. Our eyes are able to detect a narrow band of wavelengths in the middle of the spectrum. Electromagnetic waves with different wavelengths are invisible to us—but just as real. As well as light, the electromagnetic spectrum includes radio waves, infrared heat waves, X-rays, and gamma rays.

> Light that appears white is a combination of wavelengths from red to violet light. Bright sunlight looks white.

## Ultraviolet

This invisible radiation appears next to violet light in the spectrum. That is why it is called ultraviolet (meaning beyond violet) or UV. UV has a shorter wavelength and carries more energy than the light we see. The UV rays in strong sunlight can burn a person's skin, causing sunburn.

Some paints and dyes glow when UV radiation shines on them.

## Radio Waves

Radio waves have very long wavelengths compared to light. They carry only small amounts of energy, which makes them safe to use for communications. Radio and TV signals are both broadcast as radio waves. Microwaves have a shorter wavelength than radio. They are used in telecommunications and in microwave ovens. The energy from a microwave is absorbed by the water in food. That heats the water, which heats the food around it.

Radio waves carry signals between walkie-talkies as well as between phones.

This Scottish physicist was the first person to explain how light and other electromagnetic radiation works. In 1865, he said that radiation is made of waves running through the electrical and magnetic force fields that fill the whole of space. Maxwell's achievements in this area are as important as those of Isaac Newton, who explained the light spectrum 200 years before.

Our eyes see light of different wavelengths as different colors. Red light has the longest wavelength; violet light has the shortest. Green and yellow are in the middle of the range we can see.

Sunlight also contains invisible heat waves. These have a longer wavelength than red light and come right after red light in the spectrum. The scientific name for heat waves is infrared, which means "below red."

**DID YOU KNOW?** Gamma rays have the highest energy of any electromagnetic radiation, with wavelengths less than a trillionth of a meter.

# Interference

When two waves meet, they interact. They might combine, cancel each other out, or change direction. This is called interference. It happens with all kinds of waves, from ocean waves and sound, to the radio signals carrying phone calls and TV shows. Interference with these radio waves can change the signal and spoil the sound and picture.

Oil spilled on wet ground creates a rainbow pattern as the light waves interfere with one another.

## Adding Waves

What happens when waves meet depends on their phase. When waves are in phase, they are oscillating in sync, rising and falling at the same time. When two in-phase waves meet, they combine to make one bigger wave. This is constructive interference. When waves that are completely out of phase meet, they cancel each other out, disappearing in destructive interference.

Wave interference

| Constructive interference | Destructive interference |
|---|---|
| Wave A | Wave A |
| Wave B | Wave B |
| Wave A+B | Wave A+B |

## HALL OF FAME:
Guglielmo Marconi
1874–1937

This Italian inventor created the first radio communication systems. In 1901, Marconi's radio transmitters and receivers were powerful enough to send a signal all the way across the Atlantic Ocean. At first, messages were sent as Morse code, but later advances in microphones made it possible to send voices using radio waves.

DID YOU KNOW? A Marconi radio was used to call for help from the ship RMS *Titanic* as it was sinking in 1912. Unfortunately, the nearest ship had turned its radio off for the night.

A very thin layer of oil floats on the water. Some light reflects off the oil and other waves pass through it and reflect off the water. The two sets of reflected light are out of phase, so they interfere.

These headphones use interference to cut out unwanted loud sounds.

Some colors are removed by interference and others remain, making this pattern.

## Noise-Cancelling Technology

Headphones have a speaker over each ear. However, loud noises from elsewhere can make it hard to hear the music coming through the headphones. To fix this problem, noise-cancelling headphones record these extra sounds, then shift the wave of the unwanted sound by half a wavelength and play it back again. This playback is out of phase with the original sound and the two waves cancel each other out by destructive inference. The unwanted sound wave is gone!

# Reflection

Reflections are most familiar from mirrors and other shiny surfaces. A wave hits a surface that it cannot travel through, and so is pushed back the way it came. All kinds of waves can be reflected. An echo is the reflection of a sound wave. We see objects around us only because of the light reflected off them.

The light beams reflected from the smooth mirror are arranged in the same way as the light hitting it. That is why we can see a reflected image.

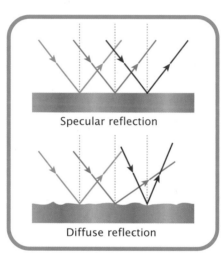

Specular reflection

Diffuse reflection

## Angle of Reflection

Beams of light always travel in a straight line, and they reflect off a surface at the same angle they hit it. If the surface is smooth, like a mirror, the many light beams that reflect off it all stay aligned—this is called specular reflection. If the surface is rough, as in a puddle when it is still raining, the beams strike it at different angles and so the reflected beams are not aligned, which is called diffuse reflection.

The radar image tells meteorologists about storms brewing.

## Radar

Radar systems bounce radio waves off objects and monitor the reflections that come back. They can be used to track planes and ships that are too far away to see. Weather satellites use radar tuned to reflect off clouds, especially those that are full of rain.

**DID YOU KNOW?** We can only see the Moon and the planets because they reflect sunlight.

This funfair mirror has gentle curves, which make the reflection look a bit strange!

The shirt looks green because it only reflects green light. The beams of red, blue, and yellow light are absorbed and not reflected.

**HALL OF FAME:**
Hasan Ibn al-Haytham
c.965–1040

This Persian scientist was one of the first people to carry out scientific experiments in physics. He made several discoveries in optics, which is the science of light and lenses. Ibn al-Haytham showed that our eyes detect the light coming from objects. Previously, most people believed the eyes sent out invisible beams that scanned the surroundings and gathered images.

# Refraction

Light travels through see-through materials, such as air, water, glass, and clear plastics. When a light beam passes between substances with different densities, it changes direction slightly. This is called refraction. Refraction makes objects appear to bend or become disjointed. It is caused by the light changing speed very slightly as it moves from one substance to the other.

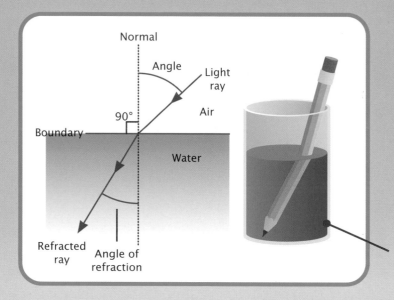

## Angles of Refraction

As light moves from air into water, it slows down slightly because water is denser than air. In this beaker, light hits the water at an angle. Since water is denser than air, the light bends toward the normal (an imaginary line at right angles to the boundary between the two mediums) and away from the surface of the water. This makes the lower part of the pencil look bent.

The angles of light beams are always measured from an imaginary vertical line called the normal. The normal is always at right angles to the surface.

## Internal Reflection and Refraction

When a beam of light hits the boundary between two substances at a large enough angle, it does not refract. Instead, it is reflected. When sunlight falls on raindrops, the light is refracted as it passes from water to air, then reflected off the back of the raindrop, and refracted farther as it leaves the raindrop. That separates the different wavelengths of light and makes a rainbow.

A rainbow only appears when the Sun is behind you, so the light can fall onto raindrops and be reflected back toward you.

**DID YOU KNOW?** Starlight is refracted as it shines through different layers of air. This makes the star appear to twinkle in the sky.

This Dutch scientist set out Snell's Law, which explains how much light will be refracted as it passes from one substance to another. It is sometimes called Ibn Sahl's Law, as it had already been described by Ibn Sahl in Persia (now Iran) in 984. Every transparent material has a refractive index that sets how much it will refract light. The larger the number, the more the light will be refracted.

Refraction makes the pencil appear to shift underwater. The pencil is straight, but the light coming from it is refracted as it passes between air and water.

Light travels more slowly through water than through air.

Because the refracted light is traveling in a slightly different direction than the light coming directly through the air, we see the submerged part of the pencil as shifted slightly to one side.

# Lenses

A lens is a curved piece of glass or plastic designed to refract light in a particular way. It can focus light rays into a narrow beam, or spread them out. A camera uses lenses to focus light to capture a sharp image of a scene. Lenses are also used for magnifying small objects or viewing those that are very far away.

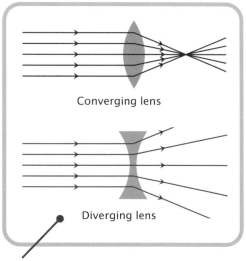

Converging lens

Diverging lens

A diverging lens can be used to correct difficulties seeing far-away things. A converging lens can be used to correct difficulties focusing on near things.

## Bending Light

When parallel rays of light hit the curved surface of a lens, they strike it at different angles. As a result, they are refracted by different amounts. A converging lens has a convex surface that bends the rays toward each other. They end up crossing at the "focal point." A diverging lens has a concave surface that causes the rays to spread out.

A single magnifying glass is good for seeing the details of small objects. The best way to use it is to hold the lens near your eye and then move toward the object until it is in focus.

## Magnifying

A lens can make an object appear larger so that its fine details are clear. The object is placed close to the lens. The way the rays of light are refracted makes the image of the object appear larger than the original object.

Your eye and brain extend the light rays along the angled path produced by the lens, creating an image that is larger than the actual object.

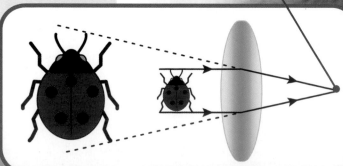

This German lens maker developed a new kind of glass that gives very clear images. Von Fraunhofer made the first spectroscope, used for examining the light from flames and stars. A spectroscope uses a lens to split light into a spectrum. By comparing starlight and light from burning substances found on Earth, scientists can work out which chemicals are present in stars.

Your eye needs to be at the focal point to see a clear image. This is where the light is focused.

Lenses can focus the invisible heat rays from the Sun. A magnifying glass can be used to start a fire, so be careful when using one.

**DID YOU KNOW?** Your eye has a lens that can grow fatter or thinner as necessary to focus light on the back of your eyeball. Its size is controlled by muscles in the eye.

# Distortion and Diffraction

Over a long distance, waves often encounter obstacles. They may bounce off the object and change direction (diffraction), or they may move around the object. If there is nothing in the way, but the object making the wave is moving, the wave itself can be distorted—stretched or squashed—as it makes its way to your eyes or ears.

## Gaps and Obstacles

A wave travels in a straight line until it hits a solid obstacle. If there is a gap in or beside the obstacle, the wave will pass through or around. If that gap is wider than the wave's wavelength, then the wave carries on in a straight line to the other side. If the gap is smaller than the wavelength, then the wave will diffract. It fans out on the other side of the gap, spreading in a circular pattern. If the gap is too small, the wave is reflected instead.

An owl makes use of how sound can move around objects as its call, with a long wavelength, carries through woodland to other owls. The call of songbirds, with a short wavelength, does not spread out.

As a swan swims forward, the ripples it makes are pushed close together in front of it but spread out behind it.

## Squashed and Stretched

If the object making a wave is moving away from you, waves are stretched and the wavelength increases. If the object is moving toward you, the waves are squashed, reducing the wavelength. The light from distant stars moving away from us becomes redder, while the light from stars moving toward us is squashed and becomes bluer. This is called the Doppler effect.

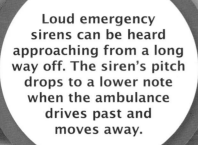

Loud emergency sirens can be heard approaching from a long way off. The siren's pitch drops to a lower note when the ambulance drives past and moves away.

The sound wave is squashed as the ambulance comes toward you. Then the wave stretches as the ambulance drives away, making the sound deeper.

EMERGENCY AMBULANCE

IN AN EMERGENCY PHONE

The Doppler effect happens with sound, light, and other types of waves.

**HALL OF FAME:**
Rosalind Franklin
1920–1958

This British scientist was an expert in X-ray diffraction. As X-rays pass through tiny gaps between atoms, they are diffracted, making patterns. Franklin figured out how the atoms were arranged in large molecules from the diffraction patterns. In the 1950s, she helped work out the shape of DNA molecules. DNA is a complex chemical that carries the instructions for making a living cell.

**DID YOU KNOW?** Doctors can use the Doppler effect to measure the flow of blood in a living patient.

# Telescopes

The word telescope means "far seeing." A telescope is used to magnify objects that are too far away and too faint to see with the naked eye. It does this by collecting light from the object and focusing it into a clear, bright image. It then magnifies that image to show the details.

The largest and most powerful telescopes are reflecting telescopes. The light is gathered using a huge, curved mirror. The curve reflects all the light onto a central point, where it can be magnified.

## Refracting and Reflecting Telescopes

A refracting telescope works by refracting light. A large lens at the front, called the objective lens, collects light entering the telescope and focuses it at the far end of the tube on another lens. This small lens, called the eyepiece, magnifies the image. A reflecting telescope uses curved mirrors in place of lenses to redirect the light. Most modern telescopes used for astronomy are reflecting telescopes.

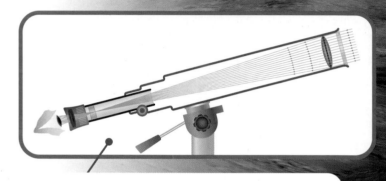

The light rays in a simple refracting telescope cross over at the focal point of the first lens, so the image produced is upside down

As well as studying stars, galaxies, and black holes, radio telescopes scan for radio waves that could be produced by intelligent beings elsewhere in space.

## Radio Telescopes

Reflecting and refracting telescopes are both optical telescopes—they work with light. Other telescopes work with different types of electromagnetic radiation. Dish-like radio telescopes pick up radio waves coming from objects in space. The waves are reflected by the curved dish onto an aerial in the middle. Telescopes that work with infrared and X-rays are located in space, as Earth's atmosphere blocks these waves.

**DID YOU KNOW?** The James Webb Space Telescope uses infrared from deep space to see more than 30 billion light-years away. (One light-year is about 10 trillion km or 6 trillion miles.)

This is the **Extremely Large Telescope in Chile, which is due to be completed in 2028. Its mirror will be able to collect 100 million times more light than a human eye.**

The telescope is designed to be able look at exoplanets, which are planets beyond our solar system.

# HALL OF FAME:
## Hans Lipperhey
*c.*1570–1619

This Dutch lens maker possibly invented the telescope. He made a living making spectacles, and then began to make and sell simple telescopes in 1608. They were used by merchants scanning for ships arriving in port, but soon scientists began to use telescopes to study stars and planets. Lipperhey applied for a patent for his telescopes, but was refused, as other people had also claimed to invent the telescope.

# Microscopes

Microscopes are used to look at objects that are too small to see with the naked eye. They use lenses arranged in the same way as those in a refracting telescope, but in a much smaller tube and with the object viewed being much closer to the main lens. Microscopes have opened up a world of tiny life forms and beautiful structures.

This mite, a tiny relative of spiders, has been imaged by an electron microscope. Beams of electrons are bounced off an object's surface to create an image.

## Parts of an Optical Microscope

An optical microscope works with light. The item being studied is placed on a stage with light shining on it. Light from the sample goes into the objective lens and from there to the eyepiece. The image is focused by changing the distance between the stage and the objective lens. This microscope has three objective lenses of different strength.

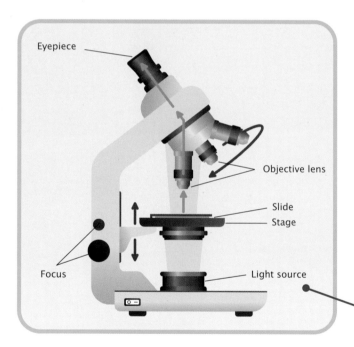

Eyepiece

Objective lens

Slide

Stage

Focus

Light source

This microscope is designed to study cells and tiny living things.

## HALL OF FAME:
### Marian Farquharson
### 1846–1912

This British scientist was the first woman to be elected to the Royal Microscopical Society, in 1885. She was an expert in natural history, especially the anatomy of plants. In 1899, Farquharson was a leading organizer of the Congress of the International Council of Women, held in London. She led a successful campaign to allow women to work as scientists and join scientific societies.

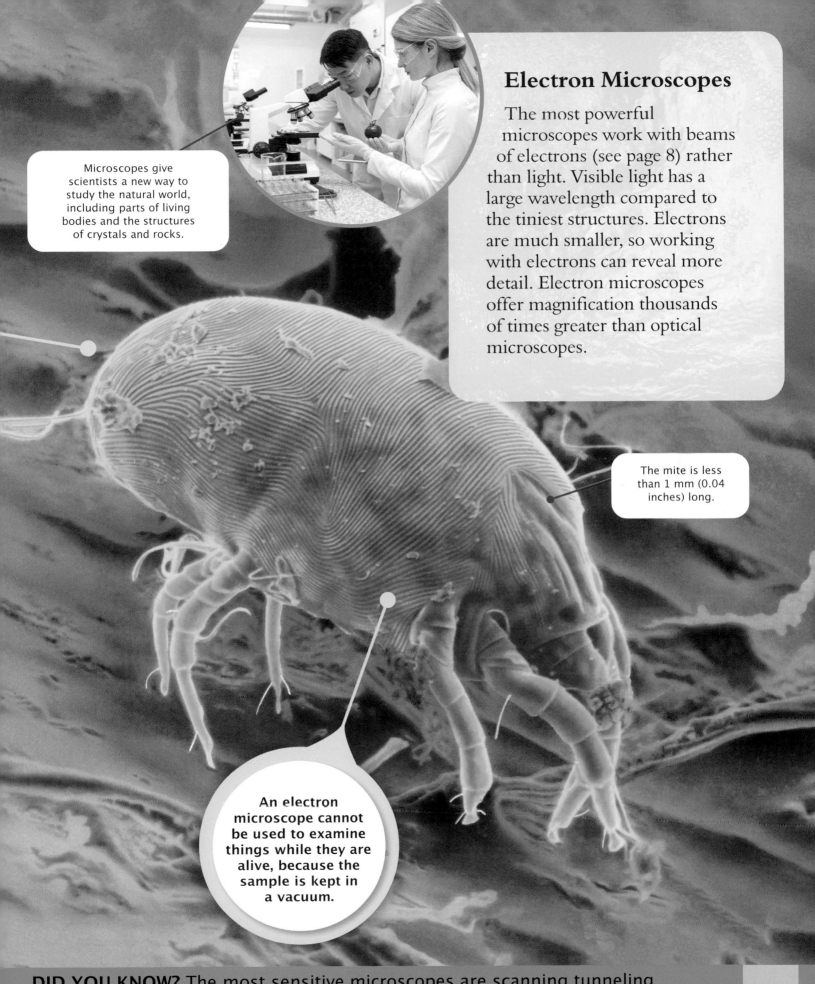

Microscopes give scientists a new way to study the natural world, including parts of living bodies and the structures of crystals and rocks.

# Electron Microscopes

The most powerful microscopes work with beams of electrons (see page 8) rather than light. Visible light has a large wavelength compared to the tiniest structures. Electrons are much smaller, so working with electrons can reveal more detail. Electron microscopes offer magnification thousands of times greater than optical microscopes.

The mite is less than 1 mm (0.04 inches) long.

An electron microscope cannot be used to examine things while they are alive, because the sample is kept in a vacuum.

**DID YOU KNOW?** The most sensitive microscopes are scanning tunneling electron microscopes that can see individual atoms.

# What Is Electricity?

This metal dome is charged up with static electricity. The metal is full of charged particles that do not flow in a current, but are static (stay still).

Electricity is a form of energy that results from particles having a charge. When charged particles move in a stream, or current, electrical energy flows and can be used to do work. Electricity is an important source of power for technology, such as computers, heating, and lights. Electricity is widespread in the natural world, too. Electrical charges carried in your nerves make your muscles move, for example.

## Moving Charge

Matter can have a positive or negative electrical charge, depending on how many electrons are present. Extra electrons give matter a negative charge. Two objects with the same charge repel each other (push apart), but opposite charges attract each other, pulling together. The attraction between a negative and a positive charge is what pulls electricity along, making a current flow.

This spark of electricity is pulled through the air because one wire has a positive charge and the other is negative.

## Electrical Energy

Electrically powered devices use the energy of flowing electricity to do work, transforming it into another kind of energy. A heater or oven converts the electricity into heat energy, while an electric car uses the energy to move. These devices need a constant flow of electricity to keep working, as the energy coming into them is converted into another form as they work.

Food mixers use electricity to spin sharp blades at high speeds that cut food into smaller chunks.

Each strand of hair has the same electric charge, so they repel one another—and create this new hairstyle.

Touching the dome transfers an electric charge to the person. The dome produces very little current, so a dangerous amount of electricity does not flow into the person.

**HALL OF FAME:**
Nikola Tesla
1856–1943

This inventor and electrical engineer was born in Serbia but moved to America as a young man. He invented many electrical devices, including an electric motor, a wireless lighting system, remote control that worked by radio, a vertical take-off plane, and a "death ray." He also investigated X-rays and radio waves. He struggled to find money to fund his inventions, and most were never produced commercially.

**DID YOU KNOW?** The word "electricity" comes from the ancient Greek word for amber. Early scientists found that rubbing amber made it give out sparks.

# Conductors and Insulators

Electricity requires electrons to move around inside a material. Conductors are materials that carry—or conduct—electricity well. This is because they have plenty of free electrons inside that can move around. Insulators are the opposite, and block the movement of electricity.

These huge cables carry large amounts of electricity over long distances around the country. They are very dangerous if touched and so are strung high above the ground between tall towers called pylons.

## Live Wires

Electrical cables are made from a combination of conductors and insulators. The central part is a metal wire, often copper, which is an excellent conductor. The electricity flows through this metal. Around the wire is a flexible plastic coating. Plastic is a very good insulator, and it ensures that none of the electrical energy in the copper leaks out of the wire before it reaches its destination. The insulating layer makes electric cables safe to handle.

The electricity in wires can be powerful enough to kill. Do not touch a cable if you can see the metal inside.

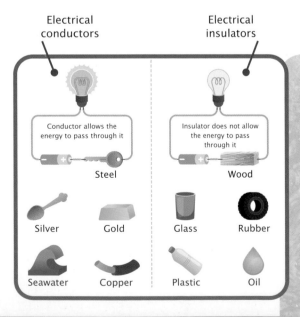

Electrical conductors

Electrical insulators

Conductor allows the energy to pass through it

Insulator does not allow the energy to pass through it

Steel

Wood

Silver

Gold

Glass

Rubber

Seawater

Copper

Plastic

Oil

## Carriers and Blockers

All metals can conduct electricity because they have many free electrons inside. Copper, gold, and silver are better conductors than most metals. Seawater is also a conductor because it contains many dissolved salts in the water. These exist as charged particles called ions that can carry electricity. Insulators are nonmetal substances such as plastic and glass. Their electrons are locked in place so they cannot form a current to carry the electrical energy.

This British teacher had worked as a clothmaker when he was young. He saw that some cloth made electric sparks as it was woven. Gray experimented with electrical charges, made by rubbing a glass tube with a cloth. He found that the charge from the tube traveled through metals and some threads, but was blocked by ivory and silk. Gray had discovered conductors and insulators.

The workers are using plastic poles to fit the wires in place. The electricity will not flow through this material.

The wires are kept separate from the metal pylons by insulators like this one made from a glass-like substance.

**DID YOU KNOW?** A superconductor is a material that conducts electricity without losing any energy at all. However, they only work this way when they are very cold.

# Current

Electricity can be static or flow as a current. Both occur when there is a difference in electric charge. Static electricity exists when there is an imbalance of electrical charge on a surface. If the surface touches a material that can carry away the extra electrons, a spark appears as the charge is instantly rebalanced. An electric current forms when a difference in charge is maintained, so charged particles flow constantly.

This ball is filled with electrified gas. When an electric current flows through the gas it leaves a trail of glowing plasma.

## Moving Electrons

The current moving through metal wires is carried by electrons. Since electrons have a negative charge, they move toward an area with a positive charge. That means the current flows from the negative (–) end of a battery toward the positive (+) end.

When the current is off, the electrons in the wire move in all directions. When the current is on, they all flow in one direction.

Free electron    Metal atom

Wire is not carrying current    Wire is carrying current

Direction of current    Direction of current

Wire    Wire

Flow of electrons    Flow of electrons

**Electric Current**

**HALL OF FAME:**
Luigi Galvani
1737–1798

This Italian scientist investigated electric currents—by using frogs' legs! Galvani was an expert in muscles and nerves. He saw that the muscles of dead frogs' legs twitched when struck by an electrical spark. He thought this was due to a special kind of electricity called "animal electricity," which was later disproved by Volta.

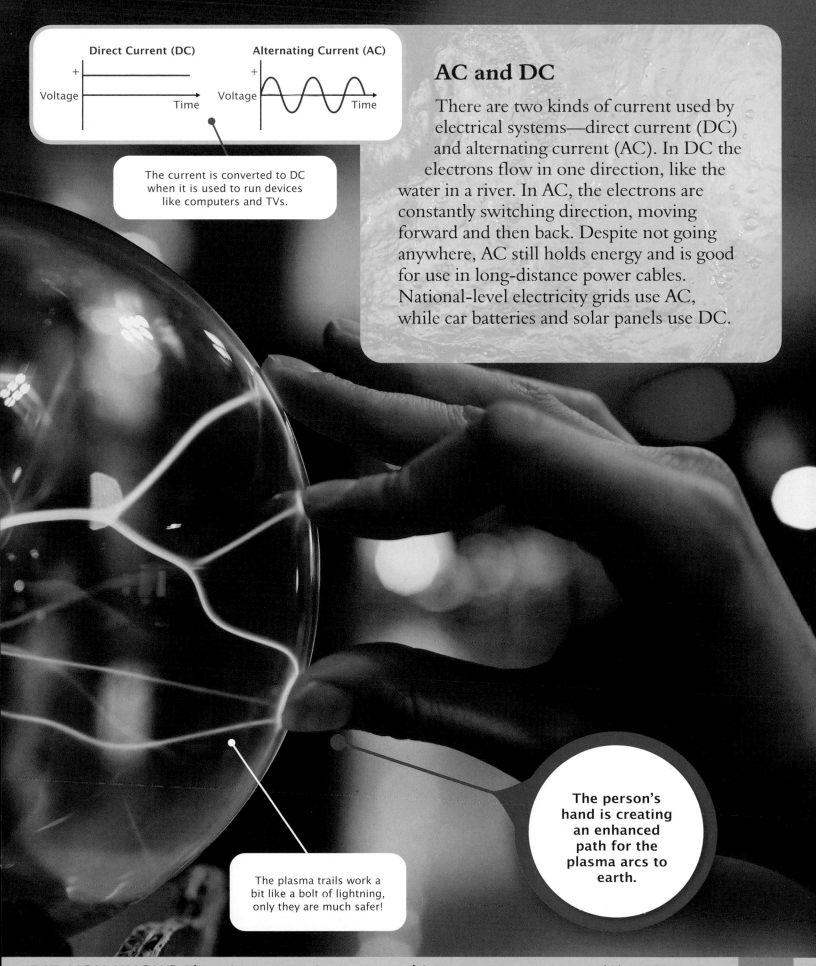

## Direct Current (DC)

+
Voltage
Time

## Alternating Current (AC)

+
Voltage
Time

The current is converted to DC when it is used to run devices like computers and TVs.

## AC and DC

There are two kinds of current used by electrical systems—direct current (DC) and alternating current (AC). In DC the electrons flow in one direction, like the water in a river. In AC, the electrons are constantly switching direction, moving forward and then back. Despite not going anywhere, AC still holds energy and is good for use in long-distance power cables. National-level electricity grids use AC, while car batteries and solar panels use DC.

The person's hand is creating an enhanced path for the plasma arcs to earth.

The plasma trails work a bit like a bolt of lightning, only they are much safer!

**DID YOU KNOW?** Electric current is measured in amperes, or amps (A). A current of 1 amp moves 6,240,000,000,000,000,000 electrons every second.

# Voltage

Just like anything that moves, an electric current needs a push to getting going. This electrical push is called the voltage. Voltage is a measure of the difference in electrical charge. When the difference is large, the voltage is high and the current moves with great force. A high voltage is needed to get large currents moving.

If the voltage is high enough, it can push an electric current through anything, even air. This is what happens during a lightning strike.

## Danger

Electricity is dangerous. Its energy can burn the skin, damage internal organs, and even stop the heart from beating. High-voltage currents can hurt people who just get too close—even if they do not touch—so always take notice of warning signs.

## Transformers

The voltage of an electric current is controlled by a transformer. Power plants make low-voltage electricity, which is transformed to a high voltage to be sent over a long distance. Before it enters homes, the electricity is reduced to a much lower, safer voltage.

Transformers are housed in electricity substations, which handle the power supply for a local area.

**DID YOU KNOW?** The loud thunder crack from lightning comes from the electricity making the air spread out so fast that it breaks the sound barrier.

The lightning is jagged because it is finding the easiest path through the air. Air is normally an insulator.

Lightning bolts are huge sparks that run between storm clouds and the ground. Swirling winds create differences in charge between the sky and the ground, which are then quickly discharged as lightning.

**HALL OF FAME:**
Alessandro Volta
1745–1827

The word "volt" comes from the name of this Italian physicist. In the early 1800s, Volta invented the first battery. He used piles of metal disks stacked with acid-soaked paper. These substances reacted with one another, creating a stream of electrons that flowed out of one end and into the other. This is the same system used in today's nonrechargeable batteries.

# Ohm's Law

The most important law in the physics of electricity links voltage, current, and a third aspect of electricity called resistance. Resistance is a measure of how hard it is to push an electric current through a substance. A conductor has low resistance, while an insulator has very high resistance.

A dimmable light bulb increases resistance to reduce the amount of electricity flowing through it.

## Electric Heater

When a material resists an electric current from flowing, the electrical energy is converted into heat. This is how simple electric heaters work. The heating element is made of a conductor that glows warm when electricity flows through it. The large atoms in the element get in the way of the flow of electrons. The electrons bump into the atoms, making them wobble, and this is what makes the element hot.

The heat given out by the element spreads into the surroundings by radiation.

**HALL OF FAME:**
Georg Ohm
1789–1854

Ohm's Law is named for this German physicist. Ohm experimented with currents from the new battery system invented by Alessandro Volta and discovered the relationship between voltage, current, and resistance. Resistance is measured in ohms ($\Omega$) in Ohm's honor. A resistance of $1\Omega$ carries a current of 1A when 1V is applied to it.

**DID YOU KNOW?** Liquid helium is the substance with the highest resistance at 1,000 trillion $\Omega$. Silver has the lowest at 0.00000001 $\Omega$.

## All Related

Ohm's Law is written as V = I × R, which means that voltage (V) is equal to current (I) multiplied by resistance (R). This relationship can be reorganized so that resistance is calculated by dividing voltage by current. Current is voltage divided by resistance. This reveals that a large current flows in conductors with a small resistance, while a small current flows in those with a large resistance.

These diagrams show how to calculate each of the three different values.

$$V = I \times R$$

$$I = V \div R$$

$$R = V \div I$$

The light becomes brighter when more current flows through it.

The resistance of the bulb and its brightness are being controlled through an app.

Home Control

# Circuits

Electric currents only flow through closed loops called circuits. A circuit connects a power supply to electrical appliances and provides them with energy. A circuit can be controlled with a switch to provide or cut the power. When a switch is turned off, the connection between the wires is broken so current cannot flow. When it is on, the circuit is complete and current flows.

**Light strings are a simple series circuit. There is one circuit running through all the lights in turn.**

## In Parallel

Circuits can connect devices in parallel or in series. This is a parallel circuit. Each light has its own connection to the power supply. If one light is disconnected, the other two will stay on as current still flows through the other paths. The voltage is the same in each path of a parallel circuit, but there might be different currents depending on the resistance of each light.

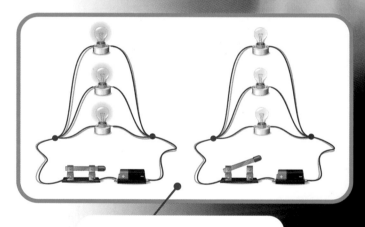

The main switch disconnects all parts of the circuit at once.

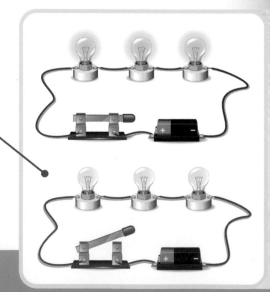

This kind of circuit is easy to create but it is not as useful as a parallel circuit. Most circuits in the home are in parallel.

## In Series

These lights are connected in series. They are in a single line on the same connection to the power supply. If the circuit is broken anywhere, all three lights will go out. There is only one path for current and the same current runs through every light.

Clarke was the first woman to work as an electrical engineer in the United States. She later became the country's first female professor of electrical engineering. Clarke was an expert in the workings of the power grid and invented a system that made in easier to calculate the voltage, resistance, and other features of the high-powered transmission cables.

This is the simplest lighting system. However, if one light fails they all go out, and it can be difficult to find the faulty one that needs replacing.

The lights are all identical and so they glow with the same brightness because the same current is flowing through all of them.

**DID YOU KNOW?** The longest single length of electrical cable in the world is 5.4 km (3.4 miles) long. It connects a power station in Greenland to the capital city Nuuk.

# Electrical Components

An electric circuit works with a wide range of electrical components. The most familiar is the light bulb. There are many other types of components that use electrical energy to perform different tasks. Switches and resistors control how electric current moves through a circuit.

A touchscreen system like this turns the display into a capacitor with a small charge stored on the screen.

## Storing Charge

A capacitor stores electrical charge. It is made from two thin sheets of metal separated by a layer of insulator. When the capacitor is connected in a circuit, a current flows into one sheet and out of the other, but not between them. This creates a charge difference between the sheets. A switch can connect the capacitor to another part of the circuit so that this stored charge flows out as extra current when needed.

A capacitor's flat sheets are often rolled up into a cylinder.

## Thermistor

A resistor reduces the current flowing through a circuit. It can be used to reduce the voltage for safety reasons. One common type of resistor is a thermistor, which is used in central heating systems and thermostats. The resistance of a thermistor changes with temperature, so the current flowing through the circuit changes as the room becomes warmer or colder.

The heating system is adjusted by the thermistor to make sure the house stays warm.

The child of escaped slaves, Latimer was an inventor with a particular interest in electricity. He designed a process for improving early electric light bulbs and oversaw the installation of public lighting in New York, Montreal, London, and Philadelphia. He also invented an early electric air conditioner, improved the safety of elevators, and wrote the first book on electric lighting.

The charge is stored in a grid of see-through conductors on the glass cover.

When a finger touches a button on the screen, a small current flows into the skin (it's far too small to feel). The computer picks up where the screen is touched and changes the display to follow the instruction.

**DID YOU KNOW?** Before batteries were invented, scientists stored electricity for experiments in Leyden jars. These were simple capacitors made from glass jars coated with metal foil.

# Light Bulbs

Electric light has changed the world. Today electric lights illuminate our homes and streets, freeing us from relying on daylight and candlelight to see what we are doing. A city's lights are even visible from space. There are three basic types of light bulb—incandescent, LED, and fluorescent—each making light using different aspects of physics.

## Hot Glow

The first electric bulbs, invented in the 1870s, were incandescent. They have a thin wire called a filament that gets very hot when a current passes through it. The hot wire glows with a bright white light. Eventually the filament breaks, and the bulb needs replacing. These old-fashioned lights are very inefficient because much of the electrical energy is converted to heat rather than light.

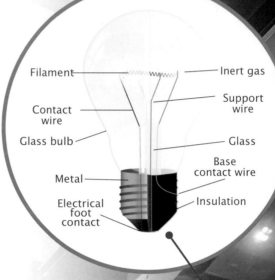

Filament · Inert gas
Contact wire · Support wire
Glass bulb · Glass
Metal · Base contact wire
Electrical foot contact · Insulation

The glowing filament is surrounded by inert gases or a vacuum that keep the filament from reacting with oxygen in the air and burning out.

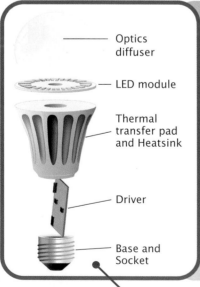

Optics diffuser
LED module
Thermal transfer pad and Heatsink
Driver
Base and Socket

An LED light is often made to look like an old-fashioned light bulb, but they can be almost any shape.

## Light-Emitting Diode

A light-emitting diode (LED) produces light as electrons move between layers of semiconductors (see page 109). Although many LEDs are white, they can also produce vibrant color and are often used in decorative displays and fairy lights. LEDs make very little heat, so they use much less electricity than incandescent bulbs.

**DID YOU KNOW?** The light bulb in the fire station in Livermore, California, has kept working since 1901, making it the world's longest-lasting light bulb.

This strip light uses a fluorescent lighting system. The bulb is a tube of gas, most often mercury vapor, which produces UV radiation when an electric current passes through it.

Fluorescent bulbs are sometimes manufactured in a coil shape to take up less space.

When UV radiation falls on a white coating on the inside surface of the tube, bright white light is produced.

**HALL OF FAME:**
Thomas Edison
1847–1931

This famous American scientist is often said to be the inventor of the light bulb. Several other people created electrical lighting before him, but Edison was the first to sell bulbs in large numbers (along with his British co-inventor, Joseph Swan). He also invented a telegraph, the first gramophone, a camera to record moving pictures, and an electricity distribution system for New York City.

# Electric Power

The forces of electromagnetism can be used to convert the flow of electricity into motion in an electric motor. The process also works the other way around. Moving magnets and conductors can be used to generate (create) electricity. Electric motors are at the heart of a lot of modern technologies.

The electric current from this charging station was generated elsewhere and brought here by the power grid.

## Electric Motor

When electricity flows through a wire, it generates a magnetic field and the wire becomes magnetic. An electric motor uses the attraction and repulsion forces of magnets to make an electric wire spin around very fast. By increasing the size of the current and the strength of the magnets, the motor can be made to spin more quickly, producing enough power to drive a car.

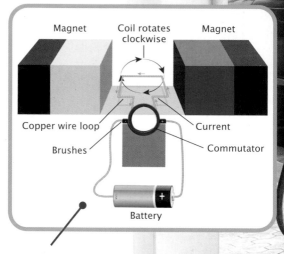

Magnet  Coil rotates clockwise  Magnet

Copper wire loop

Current

Brushes

Commutator

Battery

The ring-shaped commutator always directs the current into the right side of the wire so the forces keep pushing it around in the same direction.

**HALL OF FAME:** Michael Faraday 1791–1867

This British scientist invented both the electric motor and the electricity generator. Although Faraday had little formal education and was self-taught, he became one of the most important scientists of his day. He discovered the relationship between electricity and magnetism, and that light is affected by magnetism. He also worked on electrolysis—how chemicals in liquids can break down when an electric current is passed through them.

Many power plants use the heat energy from burning fuels to generate electricity.

# Generating Electricity

Generators change kinetic energy into electric energy. Nearly all of the electricity we use each day comes from generators. A large coil of wire spins around within a magnetic field and as it turns a current flows in the wire. In a power station, the generators use powerful electromagnets spinning inside huge coils of copper wire. They are driven by spinning fans called turbines, powered by steam produced by burning fuel or from solar power.

The car's battery uses a chemical reaction to produce electricity. The electricity from the charger is used to make that reaction run backward. When fully recharged, the battery can power the car again.

The electrical vehicle (EV) has no engine. Instead, it uses powerful electric motors to turn the wheels.

**DID YOU KNOW?** The Three Gorges Dam power plant in China can generate enough electricity each day to power 160 million homes!

# Renewable Power

The energy for much of our electricity comes from heat made by burning fuels like coal and gas. These fuels create pollution and release carbon dioxide, which damages the climate in very dangerous ways. Renewable power is made using nonpolluting sources of energy, such as sunlight and the wind.

The wing-shaped blades of wind turbines catch the wind and spin around. There is a generator linked to the blades that makes electricity.

## Solar Power

Solar energy generates power by capturing light and heat from the sun. The most common form of solar energy uses solar panels, or photovoltaic cells, which convert light energy into electricity. These are often seen on top of houses and other buildings. On a larger scale, solar-thermal power plants can produce power for thousands of people. The sun's energy is used to boil water, producing steam to drive turbines that generate electricity.

Solar panels can be fitted almost anywhere that gets sunshine.

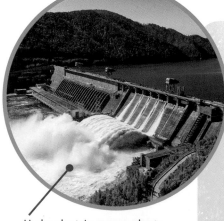

Hydroelectric power plants produce about one seventh of the world's electricity.

## Hydroelectricity

This system uses the flow of water to drive an electricity generator. A river is a natural source of flowing water that can be harnessed for hydroelectricity. The power station uses a dam to block the river, and the water is funneled through large tunnels in the dam where its flow makes turbines spin. This spinning motion drives the generators and makes the electricity.

Easley was a computer scientist and mathematician who worked for NASA. As well as helping design and test space rockets, Easley also began to figure out how the energy in sunlight and the wind could be used to generate power in a renewable way. Toward the end of her working career, Easley devoted a lot of time to helping girls develop an interest in science and engineering and study these subjects at university.

The electric current travels to the land along cables on the seabed.

Wind turbines out at sea work best because they can be made taller, and the wind here blows harder and for longer.

**DID YOU KNOW?** Solar energy could power the world. The energy in the sunlight that hits Earth each day is about 10,000 times the world's total energy use.

# Electronics

Almost every modern electrical appliance, from a washing machine to a phone, is electronic. While electricity works at large scales, with a current driving a motor or lighting a bulb, electronics works at a much smaller scale, with tiny currents and small numbers of electrons. Instead of large circuits, electronics works with tiny circuits, often etched into minute slices of semiconductor.

This display screen is covered in tiny electronic LEDs. Each LED creates one colored dot, and millions of dots create the full picture.

## Transistor

An important electronic device is the transistor. It can work in two ways. It can take in a small current and use it to trigger the flow of a larger current. This is how a hearing aid amplifies a sound, for instance. It can also work like a switch, turning current on and off thousands of times a second. Groups of transistors linked together can form simple decision-making systems that are central to how computers work.

Transistors work as switches in complex circuits that follow rules set out in a computer program.

A transistor has at least three connections. Adding a small current to the base connection in the middle causes a larger current to flow between the collector and the emitter.

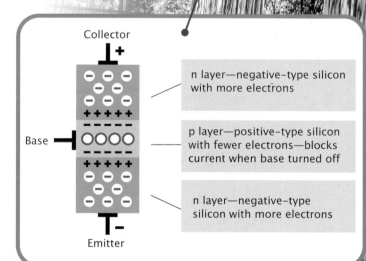

Collector

**+**

n layer—negative-type silicon with more electrons

Base

p layer—positive-type silicon with fewer electrons—blocks current when base turned off

n layer—negative-type silicon with more electrons

**–**

Emitter

## HALL OF FAME:
### Esther M. Conwell
1922-2014

Conwell was an American physicist who discovered how electrons move through semiconductors. Without this breakthrough, the computers and other gadgets we use would not have been made! A few years after Conwell made her discovery in 1945, the first transistors were constructed. Conwell was the first women to win the Edison Medal, an award that had also been given to Alexander Graham Bell (for inventing the telephone) and Nikola Tesla.

**DID YOU KNOW?** More than 1 trillion semiconductor components are made each year.

# Semiconductors

A semiconductor is a material that has properties somewhere between that of a conductor and an insulator. Most semiconductors are made from silicon, an element found in sand. How well a semiconductor conducts electrify can be changed by adding small amounts of other materials to it. An n-type (n for negative) semiconductor has extra electrons and conducts more easily. A p-type (p for positive) has fewer electrons and is less conductive. The two types can be joined to control the flow of current. Transistors and other components are made from semiconductors.

Silicon is shiny like a metal but it cracks like a crystal.

A diode (including LEDs) is an electronic device that only lets electric current flow through it in one way. It flows from n–type to p–type silicon.

In an LED, electrons move between layers of silicon with different conductivity. As electrons move from n–type to p–type silicon, a tiny burst of light is emitted.

# Microchips

A microchip, also known as an integrated circuit, is a sliver of silicon on which millions or billions of tiny electronic components, such as transistors and diodes, are connected together. Microchips are a vital part of smartphones, computers, and other devices, storing and processing information, and carrying out instructions.

## Circuits in Miniature

Microchips miniaturize the kind of circuits that would once have been wired up by hand on circuit boards. Microchips are made in high-tech factories called fabs, short for fabrication plants. The pattern of the circuit is laid out on the silicon and then chemicals are added in layers to build up the different components.

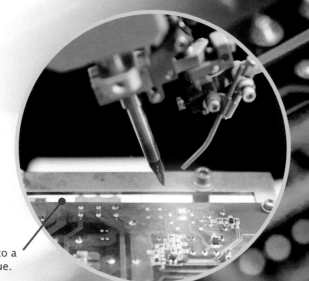

Once finished, a microchip is connected to a motherboard using solder, a metallic glue.

## Chips and Wafers

Microchips are made in sets on round wafers of silicon. The wafers are then carefully cut up into smaller squares—or chips. The silicon is very pure, and the whole factory has to be very clean. If even a few tiny specks of dirt got onto the wafer, the microchips would be ruined. The chips are made inside clean rooms, where the air is filtered so it contains almost no dust.

Workers making microchips wear coveralls and take an air shower that blows away dust before they enter the clean room.

**DID YOU KNOW?** The electronic components in a microchip are about 10 nanometers across. That is 10 billionths of a meter.

The microchip is the central processor of a computer or other device. Its job is to take in information and process it according to the instructions in the program. For instance, it might use the movements of a mouse to control an avatar in a computer game.

The microchip is just one of several components that are all linked together on the motherboard.

Microchips and the conductors on the motherboard contain a small amount of gold. Electronics should always be recycled so valuable materials like this can be reused.

**HALL OF FAME:**
Evelyn Hu
1947–

Hu is a world expert in nanotechnology, which involves making machines that are only a few billionths of a meter long. Hu works to make semiconductors smaller and smaller so more can fit onto microchips. She is also interested in making computers that do not need microchips at all, and instead work in a completely different way using quantum physics.

# The Solar System

The laws of physics work everywhere. Not just here on Earth, but across the Universe. Astronomers can use their knowledge of physics to learn about what's going on deep in space or on distant planets and stars. The closest part of space is the Solar System, which consists of the planets, moons, asteroids, comets and other objects held in orbit around our star, the Sun.

## Space Probes

Sending people into space is difficult, dangerous, and costly. Instead, scientists use powerful telescopes (see page 84) or they send out uncrewed space probes. These craft take close-up photos of planets or other objects, scan them with radar and lasers to see what they are made of, and sometimes even land on them to investigate further.

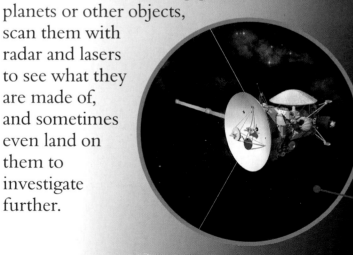

The four inner planets are small and made of solid rock.

Saturn

Earth

The Cassini probe was sent to study Saturn. The golden dome on top is a little lander called Huygens, which dropped onto Saturn's giant moon, Titan.

**HALL OF FAME:**
Mae Jemison
1956 –

Jemison was the first African–American woman to fly into space, in 1992. She is an engineer and medical doctor. She flew aboard the space shuttle *Endeavour* to study the effects of space flight on the body, including how it responds to weightlessness. Jemison was in space for eight days. After her time as an astronaut, she has worked to protect Earth's environment and make new technology safer and fair for everyone to use.

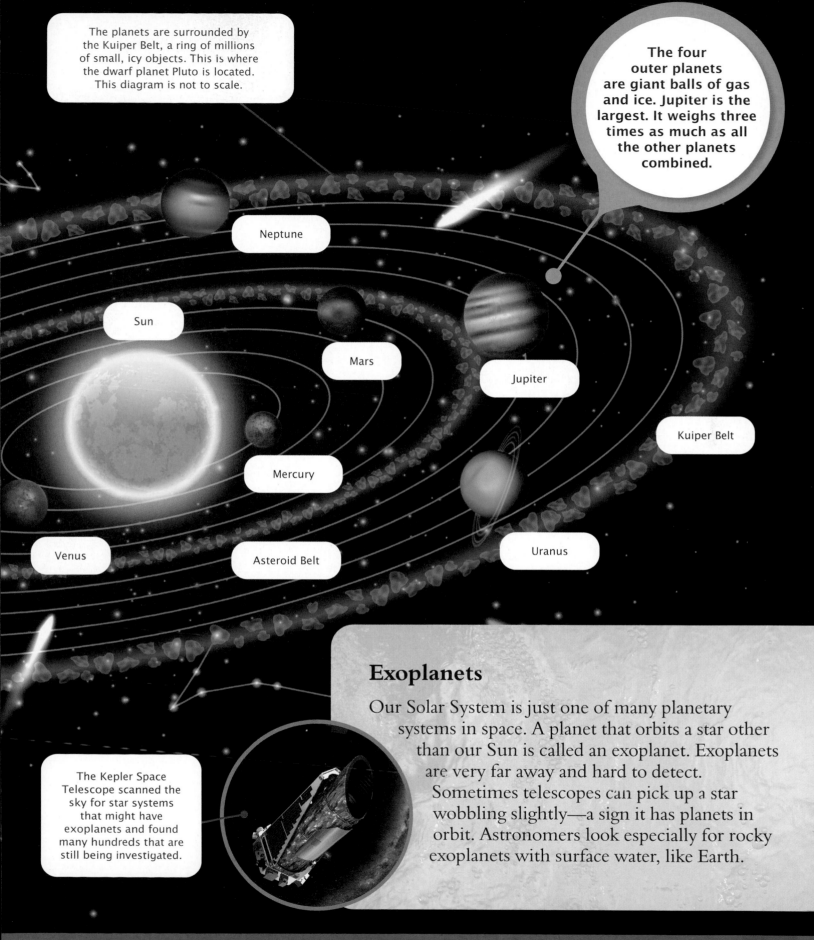

The planets are surrounded by the Kuiper Belt, a ring of millions of small, icy objects. This is where the dwarf planet Pluto is located. This diagram is not to scale.

The four outer planets are giant balls of gas and ice. Jupiter is the largest. It weighs three times as much as all the other planets combined.

Neptune

Sun

Mars

Jupiter

Kuiper Belt

Mercury

Venus

Asteroid Belt

Uranus

## Exoplanets

Our Solar System is just one of many planetary systems in space. A planet that orbits a star other than our Sun is called an exoplanet. Exoplanets are very far away and hard to detect. Sometimes telescopes can pick up a star wobbling slightly—a sign it has planets in orbit. Astronomers look especially for rocky exoplanets with surface water, like Earth.

The Kepler Space Telescope scanned the sky for star systems that might have exoplanets and found many hundreds that are still being investigated.

**DID YOU KNOW?** Astronomers think that most stars have at least two planets orbiting around them. That means there are far more planets in the Universe than stars.

# Stars

The Sun is our nearest star. It is the source of all the light and heat that keeps Earth a place where we can live. Despite being very special to us, this star is no different than many, many trillions of others. It is a ball of hydrogen plasma, which is super-hot and electrified gas.

A star is surrounded by a layer of gases called the corona. This outer layer is thin and very hot.

## Fusion Power

The heat and light of a star comes from nuclear fusion reactions happening deep inside the core, or central zone. The temperature and pressure there are so high that atoms are squashed together so their nuclei fuse. Through several steps, four atoms of hydrogen form one of helium, another gas, giving out lots of energy.

Every second, the Sun converts more than 600 million tonnes (672 million US tons) of hydrogen into helium by nuclear fusion.

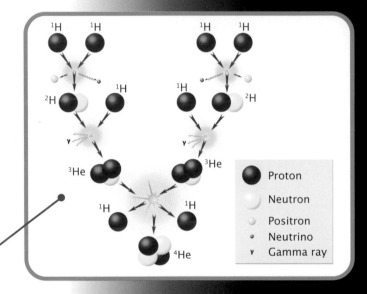

| | Proton |
|---|---|
| | Neutron |
| | Positron |
| | Neutrino |
| γ | Gamma ray |

## Inside a Star

A star has different layers. The core is where fusion happens. The energy from that leaks out into the next layer, called the radiant zone. The plasma is so tightly packed that it takes 100,000 years for the heat and light to get to the next layer, the convective zone. Here the plasma is churning like a pan of boiling water, and the heat rises to the surface, or photosphere, where it pours out into space.

Photosphere

Convective zone

Radiant zone

Core

From the surface, the light and heat of the Sun take just eight minutes to reach Earth.

**DID YOU KNOW?** Helium, a lightweight gas, was first discovered by an physicist, Pierre Janssen, examining sunlight. Only later did scientists find the gas on Earth.

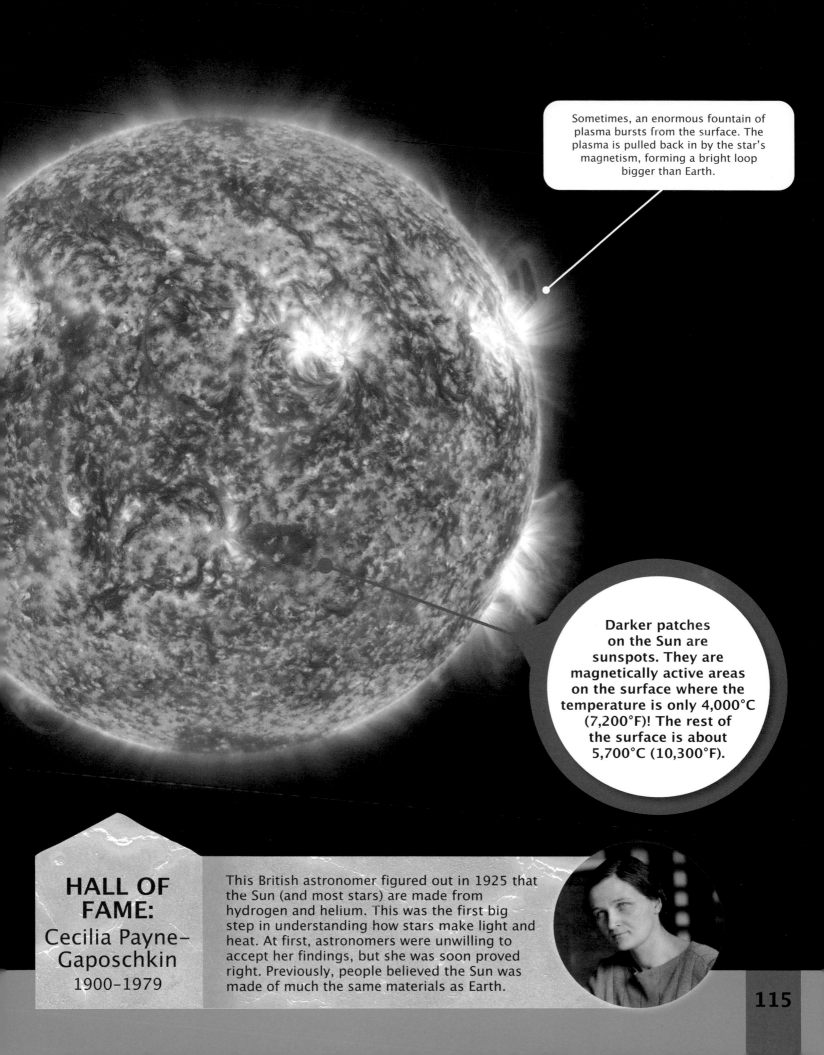

Sometimes, an enormous fountain of plasma bursts from the surface. The plasma is pulled back in by the star's magnetism, forming a bright loop bigger than Earth.

Darker patches on the Sun are sunspots. They are magnetically active areas on the surface where the temperature is only 4,000°C (7,200°F)! The rest of the surface is about 5,700°C (10,300°F).

**HALL OF FAME:**
Cecilia Payne–Gaposchkin
1900–1979

This British astronomer figured out in 1925 that the Sun (and most stars) are made from hydrogen and helium. This was the first big step in understanding how stars make light and heat. At first, astronomers were unwilling to accept her findings, but she was soon proved right. Previously, people believed the Sun was made of much the same materials as Earth.

# The Moon

Earth's nearest neighbor in space is the Moon. It is a natural satellite of Earth that is about a quarter of our planet's size. Other planets have moons, and a few are bigger than ours, but the Moon is the largest satellite in comparison to its host planet. The Moon is about 385,000 km (239,000 miles) away—a distance about 30 times the width of Earth.

The dark areas of the Moon are called lunar seas. People once thought they were areas of water, but we know today that they are low-lying regions covered in dark rock that erupted from lunar volcanoes long ago.

## Apollo Landings

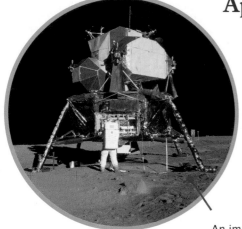

The Moon is the only world that humans have visited in space. The Apollo missions each took three days to reach the Moon. Only 12 people have walked on the Moon. No one has been back for more than 50 years, but there are several plans to return to the Moon and even set up a permanent base there.

An important job of Apollo astronauts was to collect Moon rocks for experts to study back on Earth.

## Making the Moon

Most astronomers think the Moon formed around 4.5 billion years ago when a planet about the size of Mars smashed into Earth. The planet (which has been named Theia) and a large part of Earth vaporized, forming a cloud of rock gas around Earth. This cooled and clumped together to form the Moon. Moon rock is similar to, but not exactly the same as, Earth rock because it is mixed with the smashed-up rock of Theia.

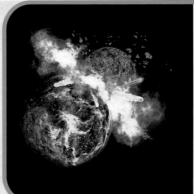
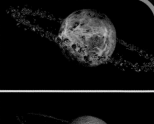

The Moon probably formed when Earth collided with a smaller planet called Theia.

**DID YOU KNOW?** The Moon's gravity creates the tides in Earth's oceans. It pulls on the oceans' water, creating a bulge on each side of Earth. As Earth turns, the bulges move around, creating high tide.

This Dutch astronomer made many discoveries about the Solar System. He spent most of his life working in the United States, where he became an expert in observing planets and moons. He discovered two moons around Uranus, and his expertise helped to figure out where the best places would be to land astronauts on the Moon for the Apollo missions. The Kuiper Belt of ice worlds beyond Neptune is named for him.

The Moon turns on its axis once for each orbit of Earth, so we always see the same side. The far side is not dark, it is just hidden from view.

The Moon has no atmosphere. Its gravity is only one sixth of Earth's gravity and so any gases it had have long since drifted away into space.

# The Planets

The eight planets of our solar system are held in orbit around the Sun by the Sun's gravity. They are at different distances from the Sun, so their orbits take different amounts of time. Neptune, farthest from the Sun, takes 165 years to make a single orbit, while Earth's orbit is one year and that of Mercury is just 88 days.

The planets formed 4.6 billion years ago from a vast disk of dust, ice, and gas whirling around the young Sun. The heavier rocky dust moved closer to the star. The lighter gases and ices drifted farther away.

## Giant Planets

The four outer planets are much larger than the inner four. Jupiter and Saturn are gas giants, formed mostly from hydrogen and helium around a small core of rock and ice. Uranus and Neptune have thin outer shells of hydrogen and helium surrounding dense icy water and ammonia and a larger icy, rocky core. They are known as ice giant planets.

Saturn is famous for its rings. These are made of chunks of ice. Although the rings are hundreds of thousands of kilometers across, they are only about 100 m (330 ft) thick.

## Rocky Planets

The four inner planets are rocky worlds. Earth is the third from the Sun and the largest, closely followed by Venus. Mars is about half this size, while Mercury, the smallest planet, is a third of Earth's size. Conditions on the rocky planets vary a lot. Mercury and Venus are scorchingly hot, while Mars is a cold, dry place. Earth is the only planet where liquid water always exists on the surface.

Mars looks red even when seen with the naked eye. The red comes from the iron-rich sand and rocks that cover the planet.

As the planets grew, their gravity swept up the gas, dust, and ice, leaving the empty space we see today

The planets grew through collisions. Smaller lumps of rock bumped into each other and stuck together. Gradually the planets grew bigger and bigger, becoming round as gravity pulled equally on all parts of their surface.

**HALL OF FAME:**
Moogega Cooper
1985–

This American planetary scientist is part of the team that controls the Perseverance rover that landed on Mars in 2020. The wheeled, car–sized robot examines rocks, looking for chemicals that are made by living things. Cooper made sure that Perseverance did not carry germs from Earth that might contaminate Mars and either affect any Martian life or mislead future scientists.

**DID YOU KNOW?** At least nine rocky bodies that do not quite qualify as planets are called dwarf planets. Most lie far beyond Neptune. Pluto, the largest of the dwarf planets, is about a third the size of Earth's Moon

# Comets and Asteroids

In addition to the planets, the Solar System has many millions of smaller objects. The inner Solar System has asteroids made of a mixture of rock, metals, and some ice. Comets come from the cold outer Solar System and are made of ices mixed with rock dust. The many craters we see on the Moon are evidence of asteroids and comets crashing into it long ago. Others have hit Earth.

## Asteroids

Most asteroids orbit in the Asteroid Belt, which is a vast ring of rocks that circles the Sun between the orbits of Mars and Jupiter. The largest object in the asteroid belt is the dwarf planet Ceres, which is about 940 km (584 miles) across.

Asteroids contain the same materials that made the rocky planets billions of years ago.

This crater in the Arizona desert was made by a meteor 50 m (160 ft) wide.

## Meteors and Meteorites

Any space rock that enters Earth's atmosphere is called a meteor. Mostly these rocks are pea-sized pebbles or specks of dust. Friction with the air as they fall makes them very hot and they burn up, appearing to us as shooting stars. Occasionally, larger rocks reach the ground. These are called meteorites. Impacts from a large meteorite are very rare but can be catastrophic. The dinosaurs died out after an asteroid 10 km (6 miles) wide hit the planet 66 million years ago.

Although born in Germany, Herschel worked as an astronomer with her older brother, William, in Britain. Working together and separately, they discovered Uranus, many asteroids, and created very accurate star maps. Herschel's search for comets and nebulas (fuzzy gas clouds) led her to discover at least five comets.

Comets develop a tail as they approach the Sun. Ice in the comet melts, freeing particles of dust. The Sun illuminates the dust, making a bright streak in the sky.

A comet's tail is millions of kilometers long. It always faces away from the Sun, so the tail is in front of the comet as it flies back into deep space.

The lumpy nucleus of a comet looks like a dirty snowball. Comets formed in the colder parts of the Solar System and can be knocked toward the Sun by collisions. Many comets take hundreds of years to orbit the Sun just once.

**DID YOU KNOW?** The moons of Mars, Phobos and Deimos, are thought to be asteroids that have been captured by the red planet's gravity.

# Galaxies

Stars are not evenly spread through the Universe. Instead, they cluster in groups called galaxies. The space between the galaxies is largely empty, with no stars there at all. Our galaxy is called the Milky Way. It is 88,000 light-years wide. That means it take 88,000 years for the light from a star on one side of the galaxy to reach the opposite side.

Our Solar System is located toward the edge of one of our galaxy's spiral arms. When we look toward the middle of the galaxy we can see a pale streak running across the sky that is made up of the light of billions of stars.

## Spirals and Disks

The Milky Way has at least 100 billion stars, probably many more. The stars are arranged in a spiral that is spinning around a central point. Many galaxies have this spiral shape. Old galaxies that formed a long time ago are normally oval or egg-shaped. The largest galaxies, with perhaps 100 times as many stars as ours, have a cloud-like irregular shape. They are thought to be made by several smaller galaxies colliding and combining.

This is the Sombrero Galaxy, a very bright oval galaxy 31 million light–years from Earth.

## HALL OF FAME:
### Jacobus Kapteyn
1851–1922

This Dutch astronomer discovered that the Milky Way is rotating. He noticed that stars in one direction in the sky seemed to be moving faster than those in the other. He realized that he was seeing some stars on the edge of a great rotating disk and others nearer the middle.

**DID YOU KNOW?** No one is quite sure how many galaxies the Universe has. It could be as few as 200 billion or as many as 2 trillion (ten times more)!

The name Milky Way comes from ancient Greece. Today's English word "galaxy" comes from the Greek word for milk.

## Black Hole

Astronomers have found an enormous black hole in the middle of the Milky Way, named Sagittarius A★. A black hole is an area of such intense gravity that not even light can escape, making it appear completely dark. Every large galaxy probably has a central black hole. Sagittarius A★ is millions of times the mass of the Sun. Galaxies with an active central black hole glow very brightly and give out powerful X-rays and radio waves.

Although a black hole itself is entirely dark, it can be revealed by bursts of electromagnetic radiation from things being pulled into it.

The Milky Way has different names around the world. In China it is the Silver River, and the Vikings called it the World Tree. The Aboriginal people of northern Australia see it as a colony of termites.

# Space and Time

Odd things happen when you travel at the speed of light. Objects become more massive and grow shorter. Time passes more slowly. The laws of physics of Newton and others don't seem to work anymore. It took perhaps the world's greatest physicist, Albert Einstein, to explain why this is, with his famous (and complicated) theory of relativity. Einstein's theory joins space, time, and energy together to explain why the speed of light is always the same and how gravity really works.

Einstein's theory also says that mass bends, or warps, space. Space warps around planets and stars, creating gravity.

## Speed of Light

The traditional laws of motion say that a light beam shining out of a rocket should be moving at the speed of light, plus the speed of the rocket. But when physicists measure light, it is always the same speed, regardless of where it comes from! It is a law of physics that light always moves at the same speed in a vacuum—nearly 300,000 km per second) (186,000 miles per second).

What would you see if you sat on a beam of light whizzing through space? Einstein set himself this puzzle.

**HALL OF FAME:** Albert Einstein 1879-1955

The popular idea of a genius scientist is based on Einstein, with his bushy mustache, wild white hair, and German accent. Einstein was bored at school and his teachers did not think he was very smart. He worked in quiet office job and used his spare time to work on physics. Only after publishing his early theories in 1905 did Einstein get a job as a full-time scientist.

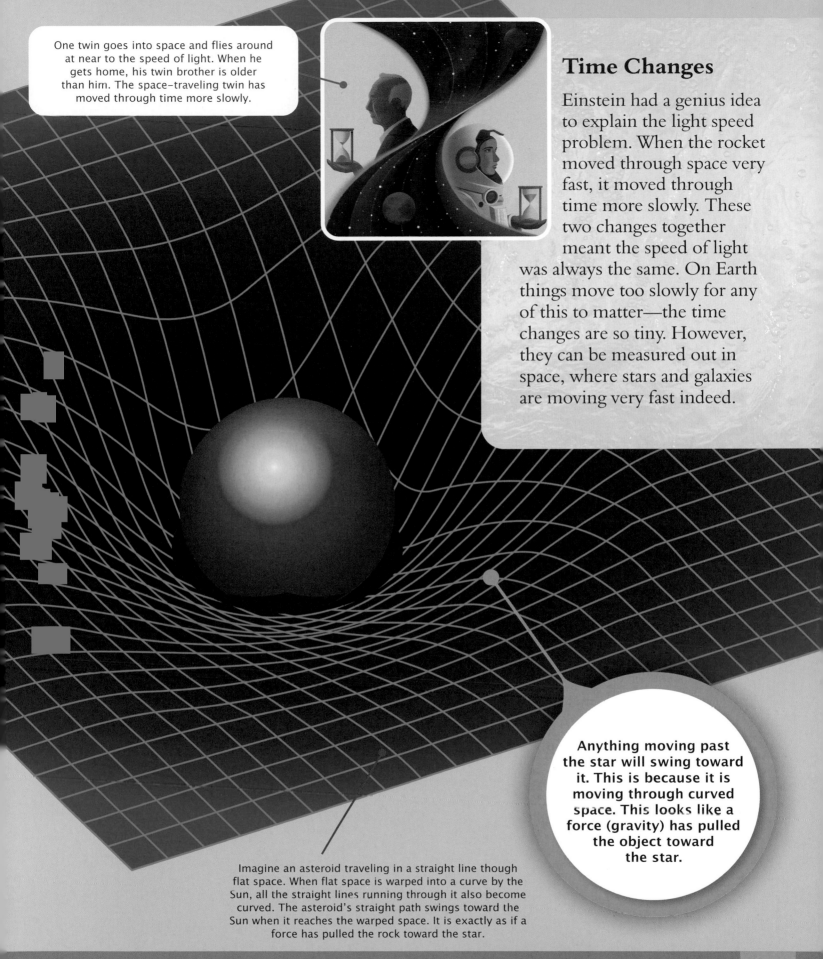

One twin goes into space and flies around at near to the speed of light. When he gets home, his twin brother is older than him. The space-traveling twin has moved through time more slowly.

## Time Changes

Einstein had a genius idea to explain the light speed problem. When the rocket moved through space very fast, it moved through time more slowly. These two changes together meant the speed of light was always the same. On Earth things move too slowly for any of this to matter—the time changes are so tiny. However, they can be measured out in space, where stars and galaxies are moving very fast indeed.

Anything moving past the star will swing toward it. This is because it is moving through curved space. This looks like a force (gravity) has pulled the object toward the star.

Imagine an asteroid traveling in a straight line though flat space. When flat space is warped into a curve by the Sun, all the straight lines running through it also become curved. The asteroid's straight path swings toward the Sun when it reaches the warped space. It is exactly as if a force has pulled the rock toward the star.

**DID YOU KNOW?** People living on the ground floor of a tall building age more slowly (by a billionth of a second or so) than the people living on the top floor.

# Glossary

**ACCELERATION**
How quickly an object changes its speed, either getting faster or slowing down, and its direction.

**AIR RESISTANCE**
The force that pushes against an object as it moves through air.

**AMPLITUDE**
The height (or depth) of a wave measured from the middle.

**ATOM**
A tiny particle that is a building block of matter.

**ATTRACT**
To cause something to move towards something else.

**BLACK HOLE**
An object in space that is so dense that light cannot escape the pull of its gravity.

**BUOYANT**
Able to float.

**CONDUCTION**
The movement of heat or electricity through a substance.

**CONVECTION**
The transfer of heat through a liquid or gas due to moving currents created by hot material rising and cold material sinking.

**DIFFRACTION**
When a wave spreads out in after it travels through a gap.

**DRAG**
Another name for air resistance, or water resistance, experienced bean object moving through a liquid or gas, such as water or air.

**ELECTRIC CURRENT**
A flow of particles that carry an electric charge.

**ELECTRICITY**
The effects caused by the presence and movement of electric charges.

**ELECTROMAGNETISM**
The force that works between charged objects. Opposite charges attract each other, while like ones repel each other. Electricity and magnetism are two aspects of electromagnetism.

**ELECTRON**
One of the three main particles that make up an atom. It has a negative charge.

**ENERGY**
The ability to do work that can be stored and transferred in different ways.

**ENGINEER**
A person who designs and builds machines and structures.

**FORCE**
A push or a pull that can change the movement or shape of an object.

**FREQUENCY**
The number of waves that pass a point every second.

**FRICTION**
A force that resists the movement of objects that are in contact with each other.

**GALAXY**
A large group of stars held together by gravity.

**GENERATOR**
A machine that can convert kinetic energy into electricity.

**GRAVITY**
A force of attraction between all objects that have mass.

**INSULATOR**
A substance that does not conduct electricity or heat easily.

**KINETIC**
Relating to motion.

**MAGNETISM**
The property of some materials, such as iron, to attract or repel similar materials.

**MAGNIFY**
To make something appear larger than it is.

**MASS**
The amount of matter in an object.

**MATTER**
Something that has mass and takes up space.

**MOMENTUM**
The tendency of an object to keep on moving It is calculated by multiplying the mass of the object by its velocity.

**NEBULA**
A cloud of gas and dust in space.

**NEUTRON**
A particle with no electric charge, found in the nucleus of most atoms

**NEWTON**
The unit of force.

**NUCLEAR FISSION**
A process in which the nucleus of an atom splits into two smaller nuclei, releasing energy as it does so.

**NUCLEAR FUSION**
A reaction when two nuclei join together to form a single, bigger nucleus, releasing energy in the process.

**NUCLEUS**
The central part of an atom, made up of protons and neutrons.

**OPTICS**
The study of how rays of light behave.

**ORBIT**
The path of a body around a more massive body such as that of the Moon around the Earth or the Earth around the Sun.

**PARTICLE**
A tiny unit of matter.

**PHOTON**
A particle of light that transmits electromagnetic force from one place to another. A photon has no mass or electric charge.

**PITCH**
A measure of how high or low a sound is.

**POTENTIAL ENERGY**
Energy stored inside matter.

**POWER**
A measure of how fast work is being done and energy being used.

**PRESSURE**
The amount of force acting over an area.

**PROTON**
A particle with a positive charge, found in an atom's nucleus.

**QUANTUM PHYSICS**
The branch of physics that studies how things work at the scale of atoms and even smaller

**QUARK**
A type of subatomic particle from which protons and neutrons are made.

**RADIATION**
An electromagnetic wave or a stream of particles that comes from a radioactive source.

**REFLECTION**
The change of direction of a wave when it bounces off a barrier.

**REFRACTION**
The change in direction of a wave when it moves from one material to another, such as when light moves from air into water.

**RELATIVITY**
A set of ideas in physics that explains how space and time are linked. Energy moving through space makes it bend into a different shape and time to change its speed.

**RENEWABLE ENERGY**
Energy from sources that never run out, such as solar and wind power.

**REPEL**
To make something move away.

**RESISTANCE**
A measure of how much a substance blocks, or resists, the flow of electricity.

**STATIC ELECTRICITY**
An electric charge held on an object as the result of a gain or loss of electrons.

**SUBATOMIC**
Smaller than an atom.

**THRUST**
A forward push, such as from a jet or rocket engine.

**VACUUM**
A space without any matter in it.

**VELOCITY**
A measure of an object's speed and direction.

**VOLTAGE**
A measure of the force that pushes an electric current through a material.

**WAVELENGTH**
The distance between one wave crest (or trough) and the next.

**WEIGHT**
The force due to gravity felt by an object with mass.

**WORK**
A measure of how much energy is being used.

# Index

acceleration 17, 28–9, 34–5
aerodynamics 45
air pressure 22, 44
air resistance 17, 20–1, 45
altitude 40
amplitude 69
angle of reflection 76
angle of refraction 78
atomic nucleus 8–10, 12–13
atoms 4, 6–10, 13, 50, 56–7, 83, 87, 96, 114
axles 65

ballistics 42–3
batteries 12, 54, 92–3, 95–6, 101, 104–5
black holes 17, 18, 123
buoyancy 46–7

capacitors 100, 101
charge 8–9, 12–13, 88, 91–2, 94, 100–1
chemical reactions 6, 12, 57
circuits 98–100, 110
comets 120–1
conduction 50, 51
conductors 90–1, 96, 111
convection 50
current 12–13, 54, 56, 88–9, 92–4, 96–101,
    103, 105, 107–8

dark matter 24–5
density 22, 46–7
diffraction 82–3
distortion 82–3
Doppler effect 82, 83
drag 20–1, 26, 44, 45

earthquakes 69, 70
effort 60–1, 64
Einstein, Albert 124–5
electrical energy 54, 56, 88, 102
electricity 88–111
    generation 4, 10, 12, 105–6
electromagnetic spectrum 72–3, 84, 123
electromagnetism 4, 12–13, 104
electromagnets 14, 105
electronics 108–9
electrons 8–9, 12–13, 54, 56, 87–8, 90, 92–3,
    95–6, 102, 108–9
elliptical orbits 41
energy 5, 9–10, 12, 48–67, 70
    chemical 57, 66
    conservation of 53, 56
    electrical 54, 56, 88, 102
    kinetic 48, 50, 52–4, 56, 66, 105
    potential 48, 54–5, 57
    renewable 106–7
    thermal (heat) 48, 50–1, 66, 102, 105
engines 66–7
entropy 48
exoplanets 113

flight 44–5
force multipliers 60, 62, 64
forces 4, 7, 12–13, 16–17, 20–1, 26–8, 30–3,
    35–9, 41–2, 44–6, 48, 60–2, 64
    centrifugal 38
    centripetal 39, 40
    restoring 36–7
fossil fuels, burning 66, 105–6
frequency 68–9
friction 20–1, 26, 32
fulcrum 60–1

G-force 18
galaxies 122–3
gamma rays 10, 72–3, 114
gases 6, 50, 66, 114, 118–19
gears 66
generators 105, 106
gravity 12, 16–19, 24, 26, 29, 36, 40–2, 44, 46,
    48, 54–5, 116–19, 124–5

helium 46, 96, 114–15, 118
Hooke's Law 37, 38
horsepower 59
hydroelectricity 105–6
hydrogen 114–15, 118

inertia 27, 39, 40
infrared 12, 50–1, 72–3, 84
insulators 90–1, 96, 100
interference 74–5

jets 66–7
joules 48, 49, 58

Kuiper Belt 113, 117

lenses 80–1, 84–6
levers 59, 60–1
lift 44
light speed 34, 69, 124–5
light waves 5, 12, 68–73, 75–81, 83–7, 102
liquids 6, 50
load 60, 62, 64
lubricants 20, 21

machines 60, 62–7
magnetism 4, 12–13, 104, 115
magnets 4, 14–15, 104
magnification 80, 87
mass 4, 6, 16, 18–19, 24–5, 28, 31, 41, 46, 48,
    53, 124
microchips 110–11
microscopes 86–7
microwaves 5, 72
Milky Way 122–3
mirrors 76–7, 84
momentum 32–3, 41
Moon 116–17, 120
motion 4, 13, 27–39, 42–5
    laws of 26–31, 124
motors, electric 4, 56, 66, 104

neutrons 8–9, 10, 114
Newton, Isaac 17, 26, 30, 38, 53, 124
nuclear fission 10
nuclear fusion 9, 114

orbits 16, 39–41, 118
oscillation 36–7, 70–1, 74

pendulums 36–7
planets 16, 112–13, 116–19, 121
plasma 6, 93, 114–15
pressure 22–3, 44
protons 8–9, 10, 114
pulleys 59, 64–5
pumps 23

radar 76
radio waves 5, 12, 72, 74, 76, 84, 89, 123
radioactivity 5, 10–12, 50, 72–3, 84, 103, 123
ramps 62–3
reflection 75–8, 82, 84
refraction 78–9, 84
relativity theory 124–5
resistance 96–8
rockets 30, 34, 42, 45, 59, 107
rotational motion 38–9, 40

screws 62–3
seismic waves 69, 70
semiconductors 102, 108–9
silicon 108–9, 110
solar power 105, 106–7
Solar System 112–25
solids 6, 50
sound waves 5, 56, 68–70, 74–5, 83
space 5, 18–19, 30, 34, 40–2, 112–25
space probes 112
speed 31, 34–5, 42, 52, 69
    of light 34, 69, 124–5
springs 37
stars 114–15
static electricity 88–9, 92
steam engines 58, 66–7
subatomic particles 4, 8–9, 12
Sun 6, 9, 18, 39–41, 51, 112–15, 118, 121, 125
sunlight 73, 76, 106, 114
superconductors 91

telescopes 17–18, 29, 84–5, 112–13
temperature 50–1
thrust 44
time 124–5
transformers 94
transistors 108

ultraviolet (UV) 5, 72, 103
uranium 10–11

velocity 32, 34–5, 38–9, 52–3
viscosity 21
voltage 94–8, 100

wavelength 68–9, 72–3, 75, 78, 82, 87
waves 5, 68–87
    see also light waves; sound waves
wedges 62–3
weight 18–19
weightlessness 18–19, 40–1
wheels 64–5, 66
work 48, 58, 62

X-rays 5, 10, 12, 72, 83–4, 89, 123